THE RESCUERS

Paul deParrie

Wolgemuth & Hyatt, Publishers
Brentwood, Tennessee

Wolgemuth & Hyatt, Publishers, Inc. is a commercial information packager whose mission is to publish and distribute books that lead individuals toward:

- A personal faith in the one true God: Father, Son, and Holy Spirit;

- A lifestyle of practical discipleship; and

- A worldview that is consistent with the historic, Christian faith. Moreover, the company endeavors to accomplish this mission at a reasonable profit and in a manner which glorifies God and serves His Kingdom.

Wolgemuth & Hyatt, Publishers, Inc.
P.O. Box 1941, Brentwood, Tennessee 37027.

Printed in the United States of America.

Library of Congress Cataloging-in-Publication Data

DeParrie, Paul.
    The rescuers.

    1. Pro-life movement—United States—Case studies.
2. Abortion—Religious aspects—Christianity—Case
studies.   I. Title.
HQ767.5.U5D46   1989   261.8'3666   89-5610
ISBN 0-943497-54-X

To Edward J. Allen,
who deeply influenced my life

CONTENTS

ACKNOWLEDGMENTS

I am thankful first to God, who allowed me to work in His medium—words.

Thanks to my wife, Bonnie, my severest and most loved critic.

Thanks to Mary Pride, who kept encouraging this project, even when it seemed to be stalled.

Thanks to all those who submitted to interviews and personal questions, whether or not they appeared in the book.

Thanks to the many photographers who contributed photos for the work.

Special thanks to Gary Leber, Susan Otum, Bob Jewett, and Joan Mosely at Operation Rescue, without whose co-operation I could not have compiled this work.

Thanks to all who prayed fervently for me and my family during this project.

INTRODUCTION

"Ah-h-h!" the pastor cried. A thin trickle of crimson oozed from the clergyman's ear as the hulking police officer applied the pain-compliance hold under his jaw. The low brick facade of the abortion clinic under the brilliant blue Atlanta sky blurred in his eyes from the pain that assaulted his entire being. In agony, the minister of the Gospel attempted to focus his thoughts on Jesus Christ, his Savior.

Again, the officer increased the pressure, digging his thumbs in deeper under the pastor's jaw. Again came the cry of pain. But he would not willingly desert his post before the Hillcrest Clinic and passively walk into the idling police van. He passed out.

Several police officers grabbed the inert pastor and carelessly tossed him into the wagon, striking his head against the metal step of the van. After a second, then a third try, they managed to slide him across the van floor, and his head struck the fire extinguisher.

Denied medical attention in the prison hospital for five hours, the pastor was pronounced fit after a cursory examination. He was forced to walk through the jail, and he finally collapsed on the floor, unable to breathe. As he fell, the man of God again struck his head.

In the end, his participation in Operation Rescue cost

1

the pastor jail time, multiple concussions, a dislocated jaw, and a trip to the hospital (including the bills), but he felt he had no other course to follow. He felt he had to take part in it.

Operation Rescue, by fomenting a national rescue movement, will be the most significant event in American history since the Civil War—or the pro-life effort will dwindle and be relegated to a historical footnote as Christianity's single greatest failure of nerve.

"Rescue those who are being taken away to death; hold back those who are stumbling to the slaughter," says Proverbs 24:11. This Scripture was the banner for those who hid Jews and other "useless eaters" from the Nazis during World War II. Now it is the standard for those who block the abortion clinic doors seeking to dissuade women from killing their babies. These actions often force the clinics to cease plying their trade for a time and make it difficult for clients to enter the doors. Thus, sidewalk counselors have more time to change women's minds. Because sidewalk counseling is an indispensable part of rescue missions, I include them as rescuers.

Rescuers maintain this approach is completely different from the sit-in, which aspires to make a public "statement." The rescue, they say, actually saves lives that are intended for slaughter that day. This fact has been repeatedly documented. Many children in this country owe their lives to those who are arrested and, at times, brutally treated for blocking abortion clinic gates.

Rescues, pro-life activists argue, are necessary primarily because of the command from God, but secondarily because they will provide a "tension" against which they may push for laws to be changed. The civil rights laws, they point out, would not have been passed without such a groundswell—and neither will any Human Life Amendment. Rescues are the answer to the *immediate* goal and provide a possible basis for the answer to the *ultimate* goal.

Rescuers claim the distinction here is important because Christ's commands are always stated in terms of immediate goals: Feed the hungry; clothe the naked; provide justice for the widow and the fatherless; heal the sick; preach to the lost. The idea that one would start an organization to end injustice by a certain target date is foreign to Scripture—unless fulfilling the immediate goal is a means of achieving the ultimate goal. For instance, if a hungry person comes to your door, it is scripturally insufficient to merely plan to give a check to the local soup kitchen. You must feed the man; *then* you may do the other.

All of the people who are featured in this book would much rather be able to spend more time with their families and do other personal things. But they realize that to do that now would be naive and suicidal. They know that the longer Christians take to act, the more difficult and costly the task will be. But worse still, they say our orders from the King stand. Early or late, we will be judged by our obedience to those orders.

The rescuers you will meet in these pages will no doubt be called *radical*, but that is only true if one uses the original meaning of that term, that is, "of or from the root . . . going to the center . . . of something." If *radical* refers to those who do something extreme without much thought or concern, you will not find such people here, nor will you find much of that among their companions who also struggle to save the lives of babies in other ways. These people have faced the same questions and objections that you may now face—objections that may prevent you from being active in saving lives.

The Rescuers will introduce you to some of the people who feel compelled to risk arrest, loss of freedom, financial loss, and even injury for the sake of the unnamed, forsaken preborn. This is not to slight the other thousands who support these courageous efforts financially or through volunteer "troop support," legal aid, sidewalk counseling, and—most important—prayer. Behind every army stands another host focusing on the forward push.

Many of these Christians were jailed in Atlanta, Georgia, during Operation Rescue actions in either July or October of 1988. The original operation in July was planned to take advantage of the glut of media (fifteen thousand media people) there for the Democratic National Convention. It was to last only a few days, but God hardened Mayor Andrew Young's heart, much as He had Pharaoh's in Moses' time, and the conflict burned white-hot for forty days. Those who went partook of a unique act of God and were imprisoned; the ones in this book who were not actually present were with them in spirit.

Each rescuer has a unique tale; each shares a commonality with you. These are your neighbors—these are your friends—these are their stories.

PHIL TUSSING

An Answer to Prayer

The war in Korea was the peak of the news those days. A new mother paced the nursery floor, engrossed in prayer, holding the sleeping form of the two-month-old Philip Tussing. Worried, she fretted over the prospect of her son being sent off to some "man's war" eighteen years hence.

Into the black night she stared as she mentally peered into the still darker future. She saw nothing. She prayed, "God, use my son to be a saver of lives, not a taker of lives."

■ ■ ■

Phil did not know of that mother's prayer over thirty years ago as he cruised the morning grayness of Forest Grove, Oregon, in his prowl car. His high sense of justice had formed the foundation for his dedication to police work. His usual route passed by Bours's clinic, the site of frequent unpleasantness because the doctor there did so many abortions. His eye had looked narrowly upon the frantic-appearing demonstrators who haunted the sidewalk that fronted the low wood-paneled building. This morning, as Phil rounded the corner of the drizzle-dampened street, there was only a small knot of people. He saw no signs waving, no bloodied baby dolls on crosses—just a handful of praying women kneeling on the wet pavement. Instinctively, he almost stopped the car; deliberately, he sped away, shaken by the vision.

That vision was neatly tucked away in the back of Phil's mind, where he didn't notice it eating away at him. Several months later, he strode into Bours's clinic to speak with the doctor. Phil had heard that the pro-life groups had planned an event in front of the clinic, a prayer vigil and memorial service, on a certain day. He felt it incumbent on him to apprise Dr. Bours of that fact.

Standing in the hall outside the surgery, Phil quietly listened as the now informed Bours gleefully expanded on the "tricks" he had ready for the demonstrators. But what was it in his years of police work that set off the alarms in Phil's mind? Something about the cast of the doctor's eyes, the way he shifted his feet, his stance, and the gestures he made with his hands. *He's acting like a guilty man,* Phil thought. *He has the body language of someone who has just killed somebody.*

At that moment, one of the staff wheeled a suction machine out of the procedure room and to the counter next to the stainless steel sink. With dismay Phil realized that the machine contained a baby—the tattered remnants of a human being whose parts were about to be sorted and counted like so many puzzle pieces. It sickened him to know that this holocaust was happening right before him, and there was nothing he could do about it.

For Phil, that was the day law enforcement lost its shine.

■ ■ ■

The lights twinkled in the distance marking the little sleeping towns of eastern Washington. The cool night desert air flowed past Phil's cruising car as he discussed the upcoming rescue with his wife. He had been driven by the Spirit in the last few months. He saw that pro-life work was

God's calling for him. A fire had eaten him until he gave in. The blinding speed of the changes left even his mother worried about her son's sanity, but Phil was sure.

As Phil sped toward Spokane, his mother prayed fervently—again. Now, the gentle nudge of the Spirit brought her the recollection of the night so long ago. "It is the answer to my prayer," she realized with delight.

The blistering pace of revelation for Phil had set a collision course between what he was sworn to do as a police officer and what he was forced to do by his employer, the city of Forest Grove. Phil saw no contradiction in rescues. When he had heard about them, it seemed obvious that life took precedence over law.

Phil's choice had been plain to him. In his brusque way, he had simply resigned from the police force, loaded the car, and headed for Washington.

Sorting out the details, Phil realized that as a police officer, he had sworn to uphold the U.S. Constitution. A study of the document revealed that the Supreme Court had patently stepped out of bounds in *Roe v. Wade*. He felt he was fulfilling his oath better by joining rescues than he had been by wearing the uniform and performing some of the duties assigned to him by the police department.

When Phil and the other rescuers gathered for prayer in the lobby of the Spokane Methodist hospital, the surgery where abortions were done was closed for the day. No babies died there that day.

■ ■ ■

The Philadelphia morning had begun very early for the civilian Phil Tussing and the other activists who were to play their various roles in the effort. People groped in the pitch dark of the shopping mall parking lot, faithful to the planned 5:00 A.M. meeting time. The cold and drizzly day began with prayer, the dispensing of maps, and the labori-

ous movement of the caravan through the suburbs of Philadelphia. They snaked across the river and into New Jersey.
Their destination was a small nondescript building in
Cherry Hill where there would be bloodshed that day—
unless they intervened. Not much could be seen in the
dreary morning half-light on their half-hour drive to the
clinic.

The eyes of the security guard inside the abortion clinic
first narrowed with suspicion, then widened with fear as he
saw the crowd of over three hundred approaching. The patrolman in the squad car next to the drab, squat building
pulled across the street to park.

Phil had prepared himself for this day. He fully expected
that the godly, spiritual atmosphere of the rescue would remain intact. That is what he sought in rescues ever since
his first one in Spokane, Washington. As he knelt down, his
only fear was that police would remove all 350 of them in
time for the clinic to open for even part of the day. The
formerly bored patrol officer in the squad car was soon
joined by another—then another. Phil could see in their
eyes that they were reluctant to begin arrests. As a former
police officer, he understood. They were overwhelmed.

Hostile clinic personnel arrived and swung their cars
close to the rescuers—daring them to remain in place. Pulling their cars up close to the activists, the clinic staff laid
on their horns hoping that the irritation would "shoo" the
pests away. They shouted insults and threats, but the rescuers would not respond in kind. The rescuers had agreed
to merely pray and sing hymns. The frustrated officers broke
up the harassment by the staff but were then threatened
with a lawsuit if they did not begin soon to remove the
rescuers.

The large black security officer inside the building sur-
veyed the scene with apparent calm. He felt assured by now
that the activists had only benign intentions. Spending a

good deal of time on the phone, he appeared to be settling in for a long day.

Phil couldn't help thinking of Psalm 94:16: "Who rises up for me against the wicked? Who stands up for me against evildoers?" Some years ago, this Scripture had been one of the reasons that he had chosen law enforcement as a profession. That verse continually challenged him to be not just a good cop, but the best cop. It was ironic that he now stood against more evildoers and saved more lives doing rescue missions than he had in eight years serving as a police officer. "No one dies here today," Phil prayed as he continued kneeling on the pavement.

It was not a pleasant day for a rescue. The ground was wet and cold; the low gray clouds spat and sputtered sporadically. But the rescuers' comfort would be the babies' torture. The clinic staff sought any means to enter the building so that they could get to work. *No*, Phil thought, *the worst thing that can happen is for us to be moved before the end of the day.*

After four hours of threats of lawsuits and complaints from the clinic staff, police began to arrest the rescuers. It was not long until fatigue set in. The policemen were not accustomed to the heavy physical labor and rigors of pushing, pulling, shoving, and dragging away so many limp bodies. Phil could see their strength flagging. He empathized with their position. Soon officers were picking and choosing the smallest rescuers.

The rescuers themselves were not without difficulties. The wet and cold seeped into their bones. Phil's feet and legs repeatedly grew numb, then painful. A chronic back problem vividly reminded him of its presence, but he fixed his mind on the goal of keeping the abortion clinic closed for the day.

Through all the confusion, flashing lights, and coming and going of police vehicles, Phil began to notice that the crowd of rescuers never seemed to diminish. It was then that he saw some of those who had already been arrested once. After their release, they worked their way back to the flat-roofed structure from the police station. Then they would again take their places among the ranks of the rescuers.

Ten difficult hours into the rescue mission with only 210 of 350 people booked, weary police sought to negotiate with the adamant activists. Only after police promised to release seven rescuers who had been held for lack of identification would the rescuers agree to go. It was 4:30 . . . an hour after the normal closing time of the clinic. Phil looked heavenward at the slate gray sky and praised God through the aches in his joints and the numbness in his legs. No one had died here today! It was the simple answer to a mother's prayer of thirty-five years ago.

■ ■ ■

Two days later Phil was peering at the clouds through the window of the Oregon-bound jet. He was then able to assess some of what had happened to him in the past year. Cruising at thirty thousand feet over his country gave him pause to think of the hope-filled intentions of this country's forefathers and the dash of disappointment they would feel seeing it all awry. He felt it somehow matched his own feelings when he discovered that saving lives and enforcing the law were often incompatible. But still, Phil prayerfully looked forward to the time when every day it would be said, "Nobody dies here today!"

THERESA CONNOLLY

Pro-life Attorney and Sidewalk Counselor

Now this is my element. Theresa thought, looking satisfied at the young black woman who was leaving behind the Washington, D.C., abortion clinic. She was just beginning to show that typical rolling gait of the pregnant woman. The sidewalk counselor, who was by her side, was cooing about the little baby that she carried. But this was not just a matter of sentimental women making sentimental noises over a cute little one. The baby had just been rescued from the jaws of death in the form of a looped steel blade to cut it to pieces and a vacuum tube to suck up its parts. Mother had been rescued from the persistent torments of post-abortion syndrome and possibly serious physical complications from the alleged safe, legal abortion. The counselor, intent on directing her to assistance, swung wide her car door admitting her two charges—mother and child.

Surely, thought Theresa, *this was more useful and infinitely more satisfying than choking on the dust of a thousand law books and burning out my eyeballs before a computer terminal writing briefs, briefs, briefs.* Somehow, today, being an active pro-life attorney did not seem enough. But she knew the thought wending its way in through the back of her mind was not so. Certainly, her work here had vitality, but the most important single factor was prayer.

If my only objective were to save babies, she concluded, *I would be blowing up clinics. The primary goal is to do God's will.* She knew this was so, even when that meant spending long hours in drab law libraries and burning the midnight milliamps on the computer doing *pro bono* legal work for pro-life rescuers.

But since Theresa had begun with a team of other women to sidewalk counsel outside the clinic in the predominantly black southeast district of the nation's capital, they had experienced remarkable success. Each time out, at least two women were intercepted on their doleful journey to join the American holocaust. At least two babies were granted pardon for the crime of being inconvenient every time that the small band appeared outside the abortion clinic.

Theresa's work here—week after week—was drawn from her personal deep well of fear-care-pity for these women that had been dug years ago. Crisis pregnancy was no theory to Theresa—nothing to wave off with a self-righteous comment about responsibility for one's acts. It may have been seventeen years ago, but the memory of the confusion and shame dredged up the same emotions Theresa had experienced when she had then learned of her own untimely pregnancy.

Of course, even in the atmosphere saturated with the libertine philosophy of the late sixties, it never even crossed the minds of Theresa's parents to suggest abortion. That was not so, however, for the international airline for which she worked. The unwritten policy was that the company would surreptitiously fly pregnant employees to one of the Scandinavian countries and make arrangements at a clinic for an abortion. It had become routine.

If Theresa's experience had been as simple as just her own pregnancy, she would not have felt the stabbing sensation her memories now brought her. She had chosen to eschew the abortion, and she eventually married the father of her now seventeen-year-old "baby," Lara. But at nearly the same time another woman employee, one Theresa knew and saw regularly, also became pregnant. The other woman opted for the company-sponsored abortion.

Things had gone downhill from there. Her friend began to drink heavily. Gradually, the woman developed an obsession with Theresa's little girl. "My baby would be three months old now!" she would say—or six months or nine months—whichever it was. She always knew. The tragic woman continually begged to hold little Lara. Her own arms were aching, encircling *the nothing* that she had left in her life. Drugs entered the picture when alcohol did not provide the desired numbness. Theresa still recoiled at the thought of this woman's mutilated existence.

How very helpful they were! Theresa thought bitterly of the airline company as she recalled the time with pain. Occasionally, she used to hear about the woman, but it had been some time since there was any news. Theresa offered a silent prayer for the woman and continued her vigil outside the abortion clinic.

Theresa began praying in earnest for the women who were yet to come there that day. Enduring a few kicks, shoves, curses, and the occasional spit hardly mattered if they could detour even a few. But there were so many with the "no choice" look in their eyes who only stiffened themselves, fixed their eyes on the door, and walked briskly by. Their ears were stoppered against the pleas for a moment's reflection in their mad dash to regain their former selves— their unpregnant, carefree selves.

None of them even suspected the treacherous waters they now entered. Their vision was diminished by the murky fog of deceptive palaver spewed forth by Planned Parenthood, the media, and other abortion supporters. The bright promise of an instant escape from the complicated life of accepted responsibility seemed too good to be true. Theresa knew that it was too good to be true.

She knew the operators of this assembly-line death mill cranked and chugged out dead babies and empty but bewildered moms. Yet they claimed some bizarre form of concern for the health of their clients. The prohibition against smoking inside the building was a regular boon to the sidewalk counselors. It created additional opportunities to talk to some of the women as they waited to hear the staff call their names. Some came out for a furtive smoke several times.

Theresa had seen the pretty black woman on the porch several times before, and always another sidewalk counselor had approached her, only to be rebuffed by the woman's boyfriend. Of course, that was not going to discourage Theresa who moved right up to the stoop and began to talk with the woman.

"My name is Pam," the woman said nervously, and it soon became apparent that she wanted her boyfriend to tell her to keep the baby. He was unwilling. Redirecting her energies toward him, Theresa poured out everything she had in the effort to dissuade him but soon returned her spurned attentions to Pam. Abruptly, Pam turned her eyes from him and locked in on Theresa. She grasped her hand and said, "Would you please come in with me?"

Theresa's mind reeled at the thought. Her mouth broke connection with her brain, and she sputtered out an inarticulate, "Who . . . what . . . me? In there?" But Pam did not wait for an answer. She walked in with Theresa in tow.

Theresa immediately began to pray, and as she crossed the threshold, she saw the smoky interior of the waiting area. It was an eerie sight since no smoking was allowed in the building.

Someone called Pam's name. Still following Pam as though bound in the flesh itself, Theresa reached the double doors leading to the surgery.

Once there, a staff member deftly separated Pam's and

Theresa's hands, saying, "You can't come with her, but you can wait here."

How could they not recognize me? I've been a conspicuous sidewalk counselor for months, Theresa wondered momentarily, arms still bulging with pro-life literature. They were gone—double doors closed—before she finished the thought. Theresa suddenly realized that she stood in a room looking at dozens of faces. The men were openly hostile, but many of the women had a yearning in their eyes. Moving as though in slow motion, the women began to reach out to her. Literature disappeared from her hands. Other hands seemed only to want to touch her, as though she could magically impart some virtue to them—a virtue that would embolden them to leave this awful place.

This is like a Fellini movie, she thought, seeing the outstretched hands of the roomful of women. Suddenly, a screeching broke into her awareness. It was as though a veil had been lifted. The staff person recognized Theresa, ran hysterically into the waiting room, and demanded that she leave—*immediately*.

Theresa opened her mouth to object. "I was told I could stay," she started to say. But the banshee screams of the other woman drowned her protest. Theresa walked out.

Bursting into the clean air, she rejoined her companions on the sidewalk. As she drank in the light and the lightness outside, her fellow laborers warned her that she should leave. "Maybe the police have been called, and you'll be arrested!" they worried. But Theresa perceived that her running away would only serve to show the clinic staff and the clients that she was not truly convinced that her work was right—right before God.

The police never came.

The police did not worry Theresa. What she had done was right. But the question arose in her mind, *What did it accomplish?* She pondered this as she continued her sidewalk counseling. When the answer came, it was simple. *The most important thing that we can do*, she thought, *is to try to be true emissaries of Christ.*

JOAN ANDREWS

Prisoner by Choice

It had been a brilliant Florida day in late March of 1986 when she arrived at the Ladies' Center for the pro-life demonstration. Joan Andrews felt sorry for the confused officer. He, alone, had obviously drawn the short straw—abortion clinic duty. He was so young. He was standing there uncertainly in his uniform with polished boots and buttons, his badge speaking of an authority that he himself didn't hold with confidence. Protesters were milling around everywhere, crossing the parking lot, pacing the sidewalk, even trying the clinic doors. The officer didn't know which people to watch.

But Joan would not be deterred. She knew babies would die that day if she did not act decisively.

Taking advantage of the confusion, she and another woman, Clarisa, worked their way out to the back of the two-story frame building and tapped at the rear exit. The clinic personnel assumed they were clients. The staff appeared surprised that Joan and Clarisa had braved the teeming mass of the demonstration. Quickly, the staff admitted them. Horror was evident on their faces as Joan and Clarisa passed them and mounted the stairs toward the surgeries followed by two others, John Burt and his eighteen-year-old daughter, Sarah.

Joan watched Clarisa and Sarah vanish into one procedure room, locking the door behind them. She glanced back before disappearing into another procedure room. Joan saw that the young officer already had dragged John to the ground and cuffed him. The place soon erupted in blue uniforms. Joan, unsuccessful at locking the door, turned to pull the plug on the suction abortion machine. When she realized the young officer was trying to pry her hands free of the electrical cord, she said, "Help me so the babies won't get killed." But other officers handcuffed her and dumped her with the other women who were piled atop John. Eventually, they were all dragged down the stairs.

■ ■ ■

Joan had been found guilty of the grievous offense of entering the clinic that day in March. She'd been aware in the Spirit that this one would cost her dearly, but she was familiar with difficult choices. The prosecution had insisted on charging her with burglary as well as simple trespass, and the judge had concurred. Taking a tough stance, the assistant state attorney called for a one-year sentence.

"As a matter of conscience," she told the judge at the end of her trial, "I can never accept probation, community control, restitution, or pay a fine. I can only be put in jail or released. Anything else is an agreement to let human beings be killed."

His stony judicial face contorted with rage as the words, "Five years!" spat from between his teeth and seemed to rebound off the walls of the courtroom. A sentence of five years was double the maximum recommendation of the state guideline.

Joan could see that there was more here than a simple judicial decree—it was vengeance. She simply sat on the floor refusing to cooperate further with the system.

■ ■ ■

For over a year following the judge's angry outburst, Joan's only sight of the outside world of God's creation was the single ray of light each dawn that squeezed through a chip in the paint covering the outside of the only window in her tiny solitary confinement cell. The other kind of light—the light pumped to her via the faithful prayers of friends—could not be blocked. Her own umbilical of prayer continuously tied her to the light that was Life.

Joan had refused to cooperate with the system that allowed abortion and sought to ease its conscience by flinging her the bone of early release from prison. She would not assist them. The price was too high.

"The sentence the judge handed down wasn't really to punish me for what I had done," she wrote, patiently explaining to her uncomprehending but concerned friends. "It was to prevent me from rescuing children in the future, to set an example. It said that unless you repent, unless you discontinue this, you are going to be punished harshly. It said that trying to save a child's life is reprehensible; it's 'wrong.' So to me, it was a blow against the humanity of the preborn child. How can I cooperate with that?"

So there she remained at Broward Correctional Institute. The system needed a maximum security prison to try to bury the love Joan has for children.

■ ■ ■

It was after midnight on Christmas Eve when the hard heels of the guards echoed down the halls. Keys began rattling in locks, and finally, Joan's cell door swung open. She was being transferred. The tight lips of the guards clarified nothing, made no answer to her questions.

Joan had no harsh word for her escorts. They were long

accustomed to burning words from their charges. Such things were not in Joan, even at the worst of times.

Walking between guards, she stepped outside. She could only marvel at the beauty of the December night sky that held her rapt and offer praises to its Creator.

A harried governor of Florida, after receiving a deluge of mail seeking clemency for Joan, had made the politic move of having her transferred to another state's penitentiary. The institution in Delaware was close to Joan's family, and the governor's spokesperson explained it as a "humanitarian" act but carefully excised the high official from any pro-life sympathies. The falsehood from that office was that Joan was now out of the governor's jurisdiction.

■ ■ ■

During the move, Joan had stopped in a West Virginia minimum security federal camp for several weeks. Finally, she was sent to the Women's Correctional Institution in Claymont, Delaware, just a few miles from her sister, Susan, and other family members. Her arrival, however, had not been a joyful event for everyone.

Joan was placed in a cell with two other inmates—a welcome novelty for her after over a year of solitary confinement. But her welcome was soon in question. Joan's refusal to cooperate meant automatic removal of privileges, which included having a radio.

The guard boldly strode in and confiscated the precious property of the other inmate. The monotony of prison life had few diversions, and this woman's radio was a great comfort to her. Joan could see the anger on the other woman's face.

Joan was in anguish. "Why should my actions be used to hurt her?" she cried out in prayer. This was the one thing that was worse than in Broward. At least there she was the only one to suffer for her noncooperation. When the passing of a couple of days seemed to dull her fellow inmate's anger, Joan felt it was time to approach her.

Joan felt helpless and weak as she began to apologize to the woman for causing her misfortune. Joan knew there was nothing she could do to remedy the situation. One of the other inmates fired back, "Don't you dare apologize! I never want to hear you apologize about that again. We've talked it over, and both of us really think that abortion is terrible. We agree that you're doing the right thing, and we want to sacrifice with you."

■ ■ ■

The weather was typically cold, wet, and blustery on that early February morning in Delaware as Joan was led from her cell to the brightly painted anteroom of Warden Reed. *This is certainly not the cold place that Broward was,* she thought, remembering the forbidding walls of the solitary cell where she had been for over a year.

But raising her head as she entered the room, she saw her sister, Susan, changing a diaper on her godchild, Joseph! Joan could not contain herself as she excitedly snatched up the round little fellow and held him tightly.

"What a place to have the first sight of your own godchild," she said to herself before noticing that even the guards were delighted with the child. Almost immediately they all were ushered into the small but quiet office of the warden. Joan refused to surrender her tiny, squirming captive into the arms of anyone else.

The decision to rescue that faraway day had changed the course of Joan's life as she knew it would. But now she was curious. This prison didn't have the solitary confinement to which she'd been subjected at the prison in Florida. "Many things were improved here," she puzzled, "but what could the warden want? Why would Susan be here?" And looking at the little bundle in her arms, she added, "And Joseph?"

Warden Reed seemed to be an open, friendly individual as she introduced herself and commented on what a lovely child Joseph was. But she furrowed her brow in a concerned frown as she began to ask Joan about why she refused to cooperate with intake procedures. Patiently, Reed tried to explain to Joan the consequences of her choices. But Joan was fully aware of them.

It would not be easy to break through the layers of encrusted institutional defenses to explain noncooperation to a prison warden, but she was determined to try. As she cradled little Joseph, she explained what she'd said to the judge, what she'd described to countless worried pro-lifers.

Reed answered that it simply made it "hard on everyone." But Joan could think only of how hard abortion must be on the babies. Rising from her seat, the warden pleaded with Joan to "be reasonable."

Joan, knowing that she would have to let go of her little Joseph and maybe not be allowed to visit with Susan again, steeled herself against what she knew she must do. She looked directly at the warden and in a measured tone said, "Can you imagine a hundred of me in here doing it? You couldn't function. Then imagine a thousand of me. That's why I'm doing it. It's a symbolic thing now, but someday it will be a reality."

The warden replied, "Yes, but, Joan, that's not going to happen for another twenty years, and you and I don't have twenty years."

Joan answered quietly, "Oh, but I *do*."

JEANNE AND JOSHUA dePARRIE

Young Persons for Life

Tuesday, February 9, 1988: I am hunched over my computer, writing the book that you are reading.

"Dad, when's the next rescue?" Jeanne asked, sprawling across the bed next to her mother.

"This Saturday," I replied.

"I want to go," she said.

I had planned to participate in Operation Rescue in New York in several months—but that was me. I could handle getting arrested. Letting my thirteen-year-old daughter do it was another matter . . . or was it?

If rescuing babies was a command of Proverbs 24:11–12—if that command permits me to break a normally legitimate law—what should that say about young people? Are they exempt? Must someone be over eighteen to obey God? Should I be unwilling to risk my daughter where others have risked all?

My wife, Bonnie, and I knew this was the time. Jeanne had asked us to let her do this over a year ago, and we had told her no. We felt that both her understanding of abortion and the seriousness of her choice were lacking. I told her to think and pray more about it.

She had evidently done that. Her perception of rescues was now entirely correct.

There I was, in the middle of writing a book that I hoped would stimulate more pro-life activity, especially more rescues. How could I refuse my daughter, whom I have always encouraged to stand up for what is right? I knew she was right to ask. The Scripture was foursquare on her side—even David had been a young man when he went against Goliath, and Mary had been very young to be asked to risk a cruel death by stoning.

No, the commands of God are for everyone.

But knowing it was right did not settle that scattered numbness in my mind and the free-fall feeling in my stomach. I should be led not by feelings—not by emotions—but by that sure light of Scripture and the moving of the Holy Spirit. A queasy stomach and fatherly protective emotions must sometimes be quelled by prayer.

Wednesday, February 10, 1988

Tonight I read the first chapter of Jeremiah, not on purpose, but simply because I just finished Isaiah. That chapter contains one of the favorite verses of pro-lifers: "Before I formed you in the womb I knew you, and before you were born I consecrated you." This is in the midst of God's calling to Jeremiah, telling him of his powerful ministry involving the pulling down and the planting of entire kingdoms—a ministry he was to begin immediately. Jeremiah was astonished at the Word of the Lord and protested that he was a "youth" and no one would listen.

The word "youth" is the Hebrew *na'ar* and denotes one between infancy and adolescence. Imagine! The kid hadn't even reached puberty, and he was appointed "over nations and over kingdoms, to pluck up and to break down, to destroy and to overthrow, to build and to plant."

Thursday, February 11, 1988

Now my sixteen-year-old son, Joshua, wants to go this Saturday and rescue with Jeanne. He mentioned yesterday that he wanted to rescue "sometime," but now he's convinced that this Saturday is that "sometime." He said that he had never before realized that rescues were so serious. I guess that my agreeing to allow Jeanne to risk arrest convinced him.

Last night Jeanne baby-sat a three-month-old baby in our home. As Joshua watched the little one sleeping in our living room, he realized that three months ago this child was "fair game."

I remember teaching Joshua when he was very small— because he was a rather strong child—that he was not allowed to fight unless he was defending one of his sisters or someone who was being picked on and was smaller or weaker than the opponent. Over his early years in public school—before he started in home schooling—he had been involved in only a few fights. All of them fit the above admonition. My wife and I even had a disagreement with the school principal over Joshua. He was being disciplined at school for his defense of a handicapped boy. I guess the lesson stuck—and returned in an unexpected way.

In the past, one of my greatest complaints about churchianity was the justifiable gripe that the youth (especially that energetic group—the teens) were never given real opportunity to minister, that is, to serve others. Everything involving them seemed to revolve around swim-parties, skate-parties, and volleyball—pure entertainment. I have contended that this approach merely produced the entertainment-oriented, adult churchgoers of the future. I always believed that these children have lots of energy and actually want to serve.

As usual, the Lord had turned things around on me. Now He wanted me to allow *my* children to serve.

Friday, February 12, 1988, Lincoln's Birthday

Today I thought again about the admittedly slim possibility that the system might overreact by arresting my children and putting them in the "care" of the children's services division. But I had to realize that even should this "worst case" occur, if I lose my children now for their obedience to the call of God, I will most certainly have them for eternity. I really don't wish to consider the risks of the alternative. I often forget to look at people and events in their eternal perspective, but when I do, it diminishes the need for worry.

But I must not be lulled by any "best case" response tomorrow. The police, as they've done in the only past case, may simply not charge them. One rescue is not the war. I'm sure we all will need to do many more rescues, and the system will surely try to stiffen its resolve to stop *us*. Just as with abortions themselves, the system will pick on the most vulnerable—the children.

Saturday, February 13, 1988

5:00 A.M. Our whole family rises and prepares to go with Jeanne and Joshua to the rendezvous point where they are to meet the other rescuers at 6:30. It is typically gray, though not raining.

8:30 A.M. The kids enter the clinic with Lynn David, Judy Hager, and Linda Wolfe. This is about an hour later than planned. There is an unexpected development at the medical complex. Only one door is open, and a guard is there at a desk.

Judy takes Jeanne in. To the guard, they appear to have an appointment with the abortionist, Belknap, especially since the picketers call out to Jeanne, "Please don't kill your baby!" The guard, wishing to spare them further "harassment," allows them to pass. Linda easily takes Joshua past the now befuddled guard. Lynn appears to breeze in virtually unchallenged. Actually, the guard asks if she has an appointment. She replies, "Yes, I have an appointment with Jesus to save babies!" Confused, the guard simply directs her to the elevators.

The rescuers block the doors for over an hour and have many opportunities to talk to the women and their boyfriends. One boyfriend, who is in a wheelchair, refuses to go in but elects to listen to the rescuers. Then the police arrest them, load them into a paddy wagon and a squad car, and take them to the inappropriately named Justice Center.

10:00 A.M. I arrive at the Justice Center and wait about an hour and a half. One of the arresting officers tried to bluff me by saying it would be at least six hours. (I know that unless the state takes custody or a murder case is declared, the law prohibits them from holding minors for more than three hours.)

Meanwhile, inside the police station, one officer tried to intimidate Jeanne. He obviously doesn't know Jeanne. He didn't even try it with Joshua, who sailed through the entire process. He said, "I know I did the right thing."

On the way back from the Justice Center, I dropped Jeanne off at a baby-sitting job. It's a job she loves.

I suppose that there are going to be some people who question my competence as a parent for giving my permission for this rescue. Surely this society will see me as an unfit parent, but this is the same society that allows girls Jeanne's age to decide to get an abortion without either the knowledge or the consent of their parents.

This is by no means over. We are to receive a letter from the juvenile justice system in a week or two instructing us on how to proceed. My children will have to decide whether to participate in "diversion" programs or community service or to tough it out in the courts. Both have said that they have no wish to be "diverted" from saving babies. If convicted by the courts, they will have to decide whether or not they will cooperate with probation or risk imprisonment. I will offer whatever insights I can, and I will support their decisions.

It reminds me a little of what it must have been like for young Corrie ten Boom and her sisters hiding Jews. Of course the risks to my children are not (yet) as great and, if we stop abortion soon, never will be. But only God knows for what kind of future ministry He is fashioning them.

What our children do about abortion will ultimately determine the fate of the abortion industry in the U.S. and, in that, will determine the fate of the U.S. itself.

MIMI SACK

Following God's Command

"I don't think it's anyone's business! If her mother wants them to do the abortion, then they should do it," Mimi Sack heard the insistent voice of one of her relatives shrill from the other room. She had read the account in the paper of the incident under discussion. A young woman in the Chester County Hospital who was in a coma was also pregnant. Her mother was demanding that the doctors do an abortion on the young woman. Pro-life activists had gotten wind of this and mounted a large demonstration in front of the imposing edifice. It was front page news in the local paper.

Mimi's stomach tensed at the mention of abortion. Since her conversion to Christ four years earlier, she had discovered abortion was wrong, yet she stood speechless. What could she say? She really knew nothing about the subject. Her shame sent color to her cheeks.

Mimi determined right then that she would be prepared next time. Even as a homemaker—perhaps, *especially* as a homemaker—she should not be ignorant on this subject. She had called herself pro-choice before her conversion to Christ. Her placid acceptance of abortion was solidly based on that same ignorance. Mimi had never given it any serious consideration. Now she would give it some real study.

After coming home, Mimi immediately contacted a couple who had invited her and her husband to dinner several months earlier. She knew they were involved! They directed her to Birthright, a very low-profile crisis pregnancy center.

Mimi took Birthright's training, and she began attending meetings of another pro-life group. She volunteered to counsel for the new group. But the counseling was short-lived. It was scheduled in the evenings, and her husband, Jim, had concerns about her safety traveling at that time of night.

Almost by chance, she attended the 1984 trial of nineteen rescuers. Mimi had been aware of the actual rescue in July of that year, but she was yet unsure of her feelings about breaking the law. Nothing in her middle- to upper-middle-class upbringing had prepared her for this question. The religious life of her family during her childhood had been regular, but shallow. The idea of rescues was challenging to the more personal faith she now possessed. During the trial, she was impressed when—one by one—the defendants stood up in the imposing courtroom under the doleful gaze of the black-robed judge and boldly testified of Jesus Christ and their obligation to obey Him by rescuing. Their profound zeal prompted her to seek out direct action meetings.

"Over the course of the years I was gradually getting more and more involved," Mimi explains. "Counseling wasn't enough, so I started picketing a local abortion clinic."

But in October of 1984, while she was sidewalk counseling, there was another rescue. She watched as rescuers were manhandled like sides of beef. Carelessly, police bumped and dragged them out. Mimi stood amazed at the rescuers' faces. Joy radiated from them. The rescuers continued to pray and worship in the midst of the adversity.

That day she returned to her home moved in her spirit. Mimi talked it over with her husband, Jim. They prayed about it, and conviction overshadowed Mimi. She was convinced that this was what God wanted her to do. "Jimmy gave me the green light," she says. "I knew that the Lord would speak through my husband. It was time to put our faith into action and start 'salting' the area."

So in late February 1985, she joined in a rescue that closed down a local clinic. When she was first arrested, many members of her church opposed her activities. "You are going to ruin your testimony!" some said. As Mimi thought about this, she realized that most Christians actually ruined their testimonies by *not* becoming involved in the battle against shedding innocent blood.

Since that time, her church has gotten a vocally pro-life pastor who has been involved in pickets. The mood of the church has shifted significantly. "People are waking up," she explains, "because our pastor preaches against abortion vehemently. He's on the board of the local crisis pregnancy center. He's very involved in pro-life, and everybody knows it. So they're more supportive of me now. Before I was just considered a nut, I guess. Now they understand. But I think that's why 56 percent of Americans think abortion is okay. It's because they're not educated. It's the pastors' responsibility to teach and lead their flock, and our pastor has taken that responsibility. It makes a big difference because they're not going to listen to a little housewife."

Later that year, on March 2, during a demonstration, the abortionist managed to slip in the door. Only one demonstrator noticed, but that was enough. The woman who saw him called, "The killer got in!" So Mimi and sixty-five others spontaneously rushed to the door, clogging the entrance and covering the ground out as far as the parking lot. All sixty-six were arrested.

Jim's mother supported the rescuers in prayer as she watched the police drag Mimi to the paddy wagon. But as she watched Mimi's arrest, a new activism was born.

A Montgomery County judge was moved to activism of

another sort when he heard of the rescue. He issued an injunction against more than six pro-life sidewalk counselors working at that clinic and barred activists from entering the clinic. Local rescuers accepted the challenge, and Mimi joined a small group of rescuers who entered the clinic.

They were arrested and charged with both contempt of court and trespass. Of the fifteen who were arrested that day, eleven firmly withstood and would not agree not to enter any more clinics. The fury of the judge was barely concealed. Those who would not agree received fifteen-day sentences starting that day. The others were given seven days.

While waiting for the appeal on that case, Mimi participated in another rescue in Delaware where she was put on probation and given one hundred hours of community service. The combined court appearances have been hard on Mimi's family. She and her husband decided that they would wait to see the results from the appeal.

Impersonal bureaucratic wheels turned for a year and a half. The court cranked out the denial of Mimi's appeal. She was summoned to surrender and serve her seven days. The prospect that had loomed for eighteen months had finally arrived. This would be the most difficult part of the journey, the separation from her family.

"What would a homemaker do in a jail cell?" Mimi asked herself as the cold metal doors crashed behind her. But her husband, Jim, was busy juggling his schedule to cover for her at home. Mimi's mother-in-law took on the rest. Even her children were a comfort to her. "When I'm eleven-teen, Mom," said her son, Danny, "I'm going to go in with you."

Mimi's time in the dreary dungeon was not wasted, however, because she was able to minister to inmates about Christ and about abortion. After being shown some pamphlets, even the prisoners could see the humanity of the preborn. Several vowed never to have an abortion.

There are boundless ministry opportunities in rescue work, Mimi thought. The unready mothers and their babies coming to the clinic, the glowering escorts and clinic staff, just-doing-my-job policemen, and hope-sapped prisoners all needed the testimony that Jesus Christ is alive—and that He is laying down His life for others through His people.

Mimi says, "Really it's a commandment from God that we rescue those who are being dragged to slaughter, and you can be sinning by not doing it—a sin of omission. I just don't think sitting at home praying is enough. Fifteen years of writing letters to Congress have resulted only in writer's cramp and twenty-one million dead babies. The Lord wants us to be active. He told us what to do, and we have to go and do it."

BOB BIRD

History Teacher and Reluctant Leader

Bob's wife came home that evening to find him weeping. She thought there had been a death in the family, and in a way, there had been.

Earlier, Bob had been lying on his bed devouring anti-abortion literature when he came upon a description of a saline abortion. Bob read most of it and finally flung the pamphlet across the room and began to weep.

"I'd just read this one passage," he explains. "Babies writhing in pain. I just couldn't stand it any longer, and I lost control of myself. I could just see this incredible wickedness—how everyone is fooled by all the lingo, by all the demands for rights, by the hypocrisy of the media. The whole thing is just a gigantic trick. And all of it is being screened from us—the flesh and the blood, the suffering, and the panic that every baby must go through and the misery and the loneliness the mothers go through. It's all being hid from us. And I am going to die fighting it. At that point I'd decided I'd had it, and I don't care what it costs."

■ ■ ■

Bob had not come to his conclusion overnight. Long before this fateful evening, the energetic, high-school history teacher had been virtually unaware of abortion. But in the late seventies, sick of the political direction of the country, Bob began to take an interest in conservative politics. Yet, even this was unsatisfying. "To me," he says, "the most sensible thing the conservatives were saying was about the abortion issue."

So, when Bob became publicly active in 1980, much of his attention was drawn by the pro-life cause. But the change was very gradual—coinciding with his being drawn back to faith in God. Slowly, he came to the conclusion that his almost perpetual involvement in coaching hockey, a pursuit he dearly loved, cost too much time. He felt his tremendous energies and organizing talents were needed elsewhere. "I always had a little voice inside me," Bob remembers, "saying, 'God wants you to do something else.'"

Still, he resisted the idea of assuming any leadership role in local pro-life work. He had organized banquets for them, helped start a crisis pregnancy center, and worked on numerous other projects. But he still balked at actually throwing himself into the work full time. "A lot of people have a bolt-of-lightning story to tell about how they became pro-life," he explains. "They had an abortion or their girlfriend had an abortion or something like that. But God swallowed me up like a boa constrictor—a little bit at a time."

He and his wife were hosts for Dr. William Brennan, author of *The Abortion Holocaust*, during his series of lectures in Kenai, Alaska. Bob so admired a man of Brennan's scholarship and intelligence and devotion to the cause that he decided that pro-life would be the work to which he would commit his time. He left hockey behind.

A significant change occurred in the arena of pro-life tactics. Bob explains, "I told people, 'Look, we'll win the abortion argument if we leave God out of it.' I didn't want to say that God wasn't important. I thought the clever thing to do was to try to win the arguments with logic and medical science.

"What really shifted my thinking was Franky Schaeffer. He showed me that this isn't liberals versus conservatives. This isn't even pro-lifers versus pro-abortionists. This is the cosmic struggle.

"We're fighting the spiritual forces of evil. If we are ashamed to bring God's name into this argument, He won't give us victory. He'll be ashamed of us if we're afraid of Him. All those other things are important, but God's got to be number one. Until we make Him number one, we're not going to win."

The pro-life efforts in Alaska were embryonic. It was not until 1984 when Bob was camping with his children that he became aware that the movement in the U.S. consisted of more than attempts at legislative change. Joe Scheidler's book, *99 Ways to Close an Abortion Clinic*, was a staggering revelation. "I realized that that was what was missing," he says. "This whole movement was missing a street fight. You can only go so far with slide presentations, letters to the editor, and lobbying."

Then the fateful night occurred. Bob's wife was gone for the evening. The children were asleep, and he was reading in bed. He squirmed as he read the graphic description of the searing pain of the child burned raw by the abortionist's saline. His wife discovered him weeping over his first real glimpse of the torture of the unborn.

"I think God just gives you a little window," he says, "and you don't keep the feeling for long. But once in a while you understand how much He must be suffering. God suffers because of all the injustices that go on. We hurt Him. Still, now, the living Christ is suffering. His sacred heart is being pierced. He allows us to just get a glimpse of that once in a while so we can surrender ourselves to His will."

That evening was a central motivator in Bob's and his wife's decision to take a sabbatical for study. During the 1985–86 school year, they drove to Minnesota where their families live. He hoped to immerse himself in research on abortion and submit the work for his master's thesis. Bob was able to discover the entire range of pro-life activity and participate in a way that was unknown in his home state.

While there, Bob was invited to the Pro-Life Action Network (PLAN) convention in St. Louis. He was hungry to learn more about direct action and made plans to go. Assuring his wife that he would not be arrested, Bob headed down the ramp and boarded the plane to the PLAN convention with Andrew Scholberg and some other activists.

At the convention Joan Andrews and other rescuers spoke movingly. The cramped meeting hall did nothing to diminish the Spirit of God moving on Bob. The next morning, in the cool overcast, he found himself joined to 106 others in a mass rescue mission at a Regency Park abortion clinic in St. Louis.

Bob's heart raced as he approached the line of uniformed officers and the crazy flashing lights of the squad cars. Suddenly, the sound from a series of explosions ripped the still morning air. There was an accident where a number of acetylene tanks exploded at a nearby manufacturing plant. The police chief, using a TV interview, announced that the explosions had been the work of the rescuers. "It was just like going into battle," Bob says. "Everyone was a little scared, the police were waiting for you there, and everyone was singing and praying. Then you hear this 'artillery' in the background."

Upon returning to Kenai, Bob was more determined than ever to educate the pro-lifers of his state in the most effective strategies to stop abortions, including rescue missions.

One of the cruel ironies of Bob's plunge into pro-life activism is that his colleagues—other teachers who do not even agree with him on the issue—respect his convictions. But the hierarchy of his church has refused his offer to create a pro-life work in the church, in spite of his promises to be as moderate as the leaders think necessary.

As a result of his efforts, however, he has received tremendous support from his family, especially his parents. It was no surprise to Bob that they became more active in pro-life. His mother had fought in the Italian underground during World War II and was arrested for speaking out against Mussolini and his Fascist regime. Once she had helped rescue twenty Russian POW's who were slated for death by the Nazis.

Bob feels that the pro-life people need to "grow" in their understanding of the abortion issue much as Abraham Lincoln "grew" regarding slavery. Lincoln had begun his political career with more concern for tariffs than the black man's plight. But once educated to the truth about slavery, he acted decisively.

Bob says that the pro-life growth must also result in decisive action, including an expansion of activism. "Our big fashion now," he explains, "is that the worst thing that could ever happen to the human race is war, and that's not true at all. Lincoln understood that. He hated that war and yet sent 600,000 men to their deaths. It was all on his word—yes or no—yet he understood that the alternative was totally unacceptable. That alternative was human slavery and the destruction of the nation."

But Bob also sees the Civil War as prophetic fulfillment of the words of John Brown, the famous abolitionist: "I am as yet too young to understand that God is any respecter of persons. And that the crimes of this guilty land will never be purged away but with blood."

Since Bob's area of specialty is history, he sees in that example that God will not specially favor America. He thinks about the alternatives to the American people stopping abortion and is reminded of what Jefferson said, "I tremble for my country when I am reminded that God is just and His justice will not sleep forever."

"We're building up a tremendous debt. The bill will come due," Bob says.

He explains that God has probably had mercy on America so far because babies are unseen, and therefore, the brutality is also unseen. But he warns, "As soon as the pro-life movement pulls babies out of dumpsters and gets the pictures spread around, we can no longer say, 'Well, gee, we didn't know what was going on.' We get to the point of, 'We don't *want* to know.' And at that point I think we are going to start paying. History is given to us to study and learn, and we definitely are going to have the most horrible price to pay if we don't correct this."

For Bob, both history and Scripture have indelibly written their lessons that are ignored at one's own peril. "I'm just never going to stop fighting this," he states emphatically. "I don't care if I'm the last pro-lifer in America. They'll have to kill me to shut me up."

HENRY IRBY

From Children's Home Founder to Rescuer

Thud! Thud! Thud!

Henry Irby sat suddenly upright as the sound shattered his slumber and seemed to shake the two-story white house to its frame. Rubbing his eyes quickly, he glanced at the clock—3:00 A.M.

His wife, Elaine, was pushing back the covers as Henry threw on a robe and turned toward the front door where the thundering sound originated. "Who could it be?" she asked.

Henry just turned his head and shrugged. As his large frame darkened the bedroom door, he heard shouting. *Police* was the only clear word in the garble. By long practice, Henry guided himself through the darkened interior of the house to the drumming door. He flung it open to confront two uniformed policemen. They were taken aback by Henry's sudden appearance but quickly regained their composure.

Waving a piece of paper in Henry's face, the lieutenant said, "We have an arrest warrant for" and added some name Henry had never heard before.

"Come on," Henry said. "You and I both know there's no one here by that name."

"Do I need to get a search warrant?" the lieutenant asked taking the stance of a Bantam rooster.

"Naw, come on in."

Elaine appeared beside Henry, and they looked at each other knowingly. Both understood that this was part of the continuing harassment from the local community. Neighbors in the middle-class suburb had feared that by starting a children's home, the Irbys might integrate the area. In the late sixties in Eastpoint, Georgia, just outside Atlanta, such sentiments ran high. When Henry had first heard the desegregation plot rumor, he had thought it was funny—but not at all a bad idea.

The police poked flashlights into the faces of three of the Irbys' sons and of the five other children who were sharing their home. After the unwarranted intrusion, Henry ushered the scowling officers to the door, locked up, and returned to his room.

Sitting on the end of the bed, Henry and Elaine looked at each other and sighed. They could have said it in unison, they had said it so often before, "I wonder what's next?"

This was the common refrain in the Irby home. Life had always been exciting for them. They had cultivated a wry humor about the twists and turns. Their eleven sons had provided their share of the surprises, and adding the kids they took in as a children's home only compounded that. The way they had begun the Calvary Temple Children's Home seemed a fluke, though Henry and Elaine knew better. It was their ministry from their Savior's hands.

Henry had been well into his thirties when he met Christ. Life had been eventful until then, but now there was real direction to the adventure. One day, without preamble, his pastor had asked if Henry would take in a couple of children who needed homes. Henry agreed instantly. From then on, it became an official ministry of the church.

After four years with the children's home, Henry moved

to an inner-city outreach with a special emphasis on youth. As director of Go Ye For Christ Ministry (which he still directs today) in the early seventies, he was once surrounded by a sea of angry faces from the infamous Black Panther party who were going to test whether or not God would strike them all if they touched the Lord's anointed. Henry and Elaine faced gangs, guns, and knives together. *I wonder what's next?* he thought at the time.

In the early seventies, with the ghetto still frothing, Henry was propelled into the political arena as well. He became a foot soldier in the battle to defeat the Equal Rights Amendment (ERA). In the ERA there was a joining of the forces that threatened to drag the U.S. into the quicksands of history. The horror of abortion, which he calls aborticide, confronted him for the first time during the ERA battle. "Aborticide is the basis of God's judgment on America," he says, "because the blood cries out from the ground."

This is a long way from, "Naw, it couldn't happen"—that was Henry's first reaction to the infamous *Roe v. Wade* decision. Henry and Elaine see abortion as *the* pivotal issue.

It was raining buckets on that afternoon in Pensacola, Florida, 1986. Henry sat drenched on the platform at the Thanksgiving Day rally to free the jailed pro-life activist, Joan Andrews. Randy Terry, with his bushy hair and camouflage clothing, wildly gestured and paced the stage. Terry sounded an assembly. "Do it for the babies—for America— for God!" he cried. Randy called for massive rescues in New York, Philadelphia, and other major cities. His plan was called Operation Rescue.

You've got to be kidding! Henry thought. *This guy is from somewhere in outer space. He's off the wall.*

Henry had heard of rescues prior to this rainy Florida rally. The rally itself was focused on the rescuer, Joan Andrews. *That's just for a few kooks or special people,* Henry thought. He didn't take Terry's ranting too seriously until appeals from Operation Rescue began arriving in the mail about a year later.

Slowly, Henry began to see the value of such a plan. When Operation Rescue came to Atlanta, Georgia, in July 1988 during the Democratic National Convention, he was prepared to help, but not to rescue.

Henry, his wife, and two of his sons attended the rally on the night before the rescue. "I had no intention of getting involved in the rescues," he says.

Randy Terry spoke again—this time introducing the tactic of giving the arresting officers the name "Baby John Doe" or "Baby Jane Doe" in solidarity with the nameless preborn. This, Terry explained, would probably result in their imprisonment until true names were given. He was seeking those who would hold out on giving their names. "How many can commit themselves to one day in jail?" he asked. Many raised their hands. "Two days?" Terry persisted. The numbers dwindled a little. "Three days?" he called. A few more hands dropped. "Until Friday?" Terry thundered. Over fifty hands remained.

A glance sideways revealed to Henry that three of those hands belonged to his wife, Elaine, and his sons, Gaston and Daniel. *These people are crazy,* he thought. *They are going to jail!* But then Henry slipped his hand up shoulder high. "I did not have the grace of God to be arrested," he says. "I merely obeyed."

The next morning was hot and sticky. The Irbys arrived at the staging point in the lot of the Days Inn in Marietta. Hundreds of rescuers milled around praying, talking, and nervously waiting. The diverse crowd—old and young, well-dressed and casual, clergy and layman, rich and poor—had the common goal of obeying God and saving mothers and children from the disguised destruction in the medical clinic.

Soon the throng was divided into groups, and guides were assigned to vehicles. Henry, an Atlanta native, was appointed to direct a bus. The school bus rolled off the lot and rumbled down the street with Henry beside the driver in the step well. He was stimulated by the excitement of the group in the vehicle. The thup-thup-thup of police helicopters resounded overhead. Vans and cars with news logos emblazoned on them clustered about them on the highway. But he did not have the grace of God to get arrested.

Henry directed the driver to the Fourteenth Street exit, and they descended from the freeway to face a police barricade. Officers impounded several vehicles, including the bus, but Henry merely emptied the bus and led the rescuers the last three blocks to the Atlanta SurgiCenter's squat brick facade. The rescuers left the sidewalk, crossed the property, and planted themselves before the glass door.

Rescuers took out their psalters and began a hymn. Atlanta Police Major Burnette appeared and barked into his bullhorn, "You're on private property. I'm asking you to leave. If you don't leave, you will be placed under arrest."

Henry heard Burnette from his seat at the bottom of the half-dozen steps that ascended to the clinic. Police stood sweating under the drought-stricken Atlanta sky awaiting orders, their faces impassive. Henry linked arms with his wife on one side and his son on the other. Still, Henry did not have the grace of God to get arrested.

Moments later, Henry watched his wife—then his son—dragged on to a stretcher. But he still did not have the grace of God to be arrested, and he sat with his head bowed.

He lay back and went limp and continued praying. He saw a policeman's face over him and heard the voice asking, "Sir, you are under arrest. Will you walk?" Henry did not answer.

"He reached down and grabbed my right arm," Henry explains, "and I had grace to be arrested. God waited that long—because I didn't need it until then."

Henry was loaded on the white police bus with his wife and sons and waited in the stuffy interior until it was filled.

An officer brought the engine rumbling to life, ground it into gear, and stiffly bumped down the road toward the Lakewood Fairground. Henry could see the imposing building of the fairground through the metal mesh over the bus windows. Inside, police waited at tables to book the prisoners. By the time Henry approached the booking officer, he was already in the habit of rolling his eyes upward and sighing as he asked, "Name?"

He could almost see the officer mouth the answer as Henry replied, "Baby John Doe." The officer assigned him a number, extracted the remaining meager information, and sent him into the huge interior of the fairground. Cots had been set up there in anticipation of massive arrests during the Democratic Convention.

But the time passed quickly as prayer and worship meetings and fellowship blended together. The Atlanta jail system was choking on the overload. The police were unable to move the prisoners to a regular facility for some time.

Outside, the battle raged. The district attorney, the judge, and the rescuers' attorney, the noted criminal lawyer Bob Fierer, formed a deal where all the rescuers would be released on Friday under their "Baby Doe" aliases. Margie Pitts Hames, the feminist attorney who fought for "abortion rights" in the U.S. Supreme Court, assailed the mayor's office with the demand that the 134 prisoners be held, indefinitely if necessary. Mayor Andrew Young, a veteran of many arrests in the civil rights efforts of the sixties, capitulated to the forcible command.

Operation Rescue leaders promised more rescues to overload the system if the prisoners were not released, but it was not the system they were fighting any longer. From behind bars, Randy Terry appealed for Christians from all over the country to flood Atlanta. "We are no longer fighting against the courts," he asserted, "but directly against abortion itself."

Henry remembered that he had committed to remain

until Friday. "After a week in jail," he says, "I began to wonder, Which Friday was Randy talking about? . . . of which week? . . . of which month?"

The *Atlanta Constitution* opined, "Just Let the Demonstrators Loose," but Pitts Hames held hypnotic sway over the city's leadership—to the tune of up to $10,000 per day just to house the psalm-singing, praying, and growing throng. After authorities had broken up the group and scattered them among the general population, it was like sending spores of the Gospel throughout the jail system. The prisoners who had fed on one another's fellowship now fed others with the words of Jesus.

Randy Terry, now released after giving his true name, was organizing continuing rescues, coordinating them with the arrival of rescuers deplaning from Oregon and busloads arriving from Texas. A previously planned national pastors' rescue slated for Washington, D.C., was being canceled and reset for Atlanta in early October.

Henry spent forty days watching the cockroaches scurry over the peeling paint in the jail. He busied himself working for the same Jesus Christ whose work had brought him here. "It was a life-changing experience," he says.

Randy Terry then asked the nameless jailed rescuers to reveal their names and be released in order to go to their communities and churches to recruit for the coming October series of rescues.

Henry felt bound to confront the abortion industry again during the Siege of Atlanta planned by Operation Rescue. So when he attended the rally on the cool gray afternoon of October 3, 1988, at St. Jude's Catholic Church, he was ready for spiritual battle.

Henry walked past the dark wood pews to the small knot of leaders and stopped to greet Randy. Three grim-faced detectives strode up, handed Terry a warrant, summarily arrested him for conspiracy, and hauled him away.

Inside, as this news spread, the rescuers were frozen in

shock, but by the evening rally that shock had become determination. Police Major Burnette, evoking "the will of the people" of Atlanta, had promised "gloves off" treatment for rescuers, not like the July rescues where they were carried or placed on stretchers. Leaders demonstrated nonviolent confrontation for the crowd. They taught rescuers to crawl on all fours when approaching police or going under the aluminum barricades. Randy was released on $75,000 bond late that night—in time to lead the morning gathering.

The rescuers were divided into teams under the drizzling skies. The Motel 1 parking lot was awash with stirring bodies moving toward their various transports. Henry's group followed him to the bright station of the MARTA, Atlanta's rapid transit rail line, and climbed aboard the gleaming car headed toward town. They arrived at their station to see over one hundred police standing elbow to elbow at attention. The plan required Henry to lead his crew around for two hours and converge simultaneously with other groups on the target. They walked until they were midway between two clinics—each three blocks away on either side.

Soon they moved briskly up Spring Street where the Atlanta SurgiCenter stood. They came close to the barricades that were strung like boxcars across the street. The rescuers went to their hands and knees and began to crawl around the barriers on the sidewalks.

Henry, also on all fours, could not see, but the sounds of screams and crying ripped the silence. Police had begun to use pain-compliance holds using pressure on the mastoid nerves under the ears. After an improperly applied pressure hold on Henry failed, the police, placing him in plastic cuffs, tried to lift his 260-pound frame by his wrists. Henry bellowed in pain as he was carried off and tossed into the police van.

Even the media were appalled at the brutal antics of the

Atlanta police that day. Complaints deluged the mayor's office phone lines until, it was reported, the staff disconnected the phone for relief. Later in the week, after having been videotaped kicking a rescuer who was on his hands and knees, Major Burnette reported, "Apparently the people of Atlanta want us to be more gentle with these folks."

The Siege of Atlanta ended after nine days, but under the surface it still smolders. Operation Rescue's new permanent headquarters is the focal point of pro-life energy. Henry comments, "I wonder what's next?"

DAWN STOVER

Confronting Lovejoy Clinic

Dawn stood happily at the drainboard in the cluttered kitchen drawing the peeler expertly, skinning the potatoes and watching the peelings slowly curl down to the small heap. Her mother was busily engaged in other dinner preparations and skirted behind Dawn to reach the jingling phone. Outside the overcast day reflected a sterile light off the concrete-and-wood barrenness of the northern California naval base. That barrenness was not an attribute shared by the pregnant fifteen-year-old Dawn, though she had blocked the pregnancy from her consciousness.

Dawn's attention was drawn by her mother's silence on the phone. Dawn slowly turned to a position that allowed her to see her mother, only to notice her blanched expression as she leaned heavily against the wall. Dawn immediately sensed that the subject of her mother's silent attention was her pregnancy. Her mother's hand went to her chest and clutched; her jaw was slack. Dawn froze.

Denial shaped her mother's face at first, but then their eyes met. "It's true," her mother shrieked, "it's true, isn't it?"

The rest of the day was a blur of frantic action—a sobbing sequence captured in still-shots in Dawn's mind.

"Oh, please, God," Dawn bargained through the sleep-

49

less night, "let me not be pregnant. I'll live my life for You."
She refused to acknowledge the baby inside her—already he
was twelve-weeks-old and sucking his thumb. "I just
wanted my period to start," Dawn now explains. "That's
how I thought of it."

In spite of the youthful rebellion that characterized
Dawn's life—a rebellion that had brought her to this pass—
she quickly relinquished control to her mother who now
easily led her. First, they went to the base doctor for a de-
grading examination. The doctor spoke to her mother as
though Dawn were not there. "She's pregnant all right," he
said. "About fourteen weeks along." So a week later,
Dawn's mother took her to the base hospital to "start her
period."

While on the operating table, Dawn hesitated. "I've
changed my mind. I don't want to do this," she said. The
nurses were deaf to her protest and simply strapped down
her arms. Dawn realized suddenly, "It's really a baby." But
the thought stuck briefly, only to be engulfed with her consciousness by the sodium pentothal. She awoke later—
empty.

Leaving the tomb-like hospital, Dawn turned, faced her
mother grimly, and said, "If I find out that it was a baby, I'll
come after you!"

Dawn's mind, however, suppressed any such evidence.
But a tiny person lurked just out of sight around every darkened corner in her mind. She quashed all thought of her
deed—for a few years.

Dawn strove to overcome her conscience with pleasure
seeking. Her marriage to Doug Stover lowered the intensity
of the carnality, but the root rebellion still stood. The
drunkenness and drug use continued—but on a lesser level.

A little over five years after the abortion, Dawn sat with
her husband, Doug, in the living room of their little two-
bedroom bungalow. She looked out the oddly placed win-

dow as the cold, bright autumn light filtered through the yellow-tipped walnut leaves. She heard the padding of little feet and looked across the house at her tousle-haired, eighteen-month-old daughter, Jocelyn. Newly aroused from her nap, dragging her blanket behind her, she sleepily headed for the sanctuary of Mother's again pregnant lap.

The scene sparked unexpected thoughts. *Thank God, she's alive,* entered a voice into Dawn's mind. *Yeah, I killed my first one,* she added herself.

Suddenly, the floodgates were opened and words and thoughts gushed in a torrent. "Doug," she said looking at her husband, "suppose your parents are right and Jesus *is* coming back? Suppose we miss it because of the way we're living? Suppose *she* misses it because of the way we're living?"

Jocelyn's bumbling trip across the room had signaled the end of Dawn's sensual pursuit. Her journey to Christ had begun—a journey that would lead to healing the open, oozing abortion sore on her soul and would lead to her pleading with abortion-bound women at the clinic doors.

Six months after that autumn day Dawn roused the courage to reveal her painful secret to her husband. Two more years passed before she could face the knowledge of the thousands who hypnotically followed abortion's panpipe call to "freedom." When this realization struck, she was horrified. She was frozen into inaction until she heard a pro-life couple on radio describing sidewalk counseling. Hungrily, she copied their phone number, called, and volunteered.

Her training began. Soon God had positioned Dawn as an acknowledged leader in Oregon's pro-life movement.

As rescue efforts began to blossom in the mid-eighties, Dawn eventually moved to the forefront of the movement. "I felt that sidewalk counseling was wonderful," she says. "But if it were one of my children—one of your children—

one of my neighbor's children—who was going into a death camp to be put to death, I would not stay on the sidewalk with a piece of literature."

Dawn first joined a rescue effort when she attended a Pro-Life Action Network (PLAN) convention in St. Louis, but that was altogether different from risking arrest in her own territory. She and Doug counted the cost, and she plunged in.

It was a cool morning in June when the dozen of them had filed down Twenty-fourth Street, up the three steps, and into the inappropriately named Lovejoy Clinic. The preoccupied receptionist glanced up from her scattering of paperwork and asked, "Can I help you?" In front of Dawn, Andrew Burnett answered softly, "You can stop killing babies," but she appeared not to hear. She did notice when a line of a dozen people passed under the portal leading to the procedure rooms. Her initial shock over, she hit the police call-button.

Moments later, the building looked like an armed camp. Speeding prowl cars arrived from every direction, flashing blue-and-red lights creating the bizarre landscape of a nightmare. The brilliant yellow police-line tape gave the appearance of the investigation of a murder scene, but the murders in this place would not be investigated.

Dawn was not aware of this surrealistic sight. She stared, numbed, at the chrome-steel, sanitized-for-surgery suction abortion machine. She prayed as she stood there. *Babies die here*, she thought. *I will not leave of my own accord.*

Police carelessly removed Dawn along with her eleven cohorts and drove off with the wagonload in the direction of the downtown Portland Justice Center.

For this Friday the 13th rescue, Dawn stood before Judge Amiton, and she was pronounced guilty. She respectfully informed the judge behind the bench that she would not comply with probation—that she would rescue more children. Amiton's mouth hung open; his eyes stared in disbelief. He was unable to recall anyone who had so succinctly and honestly stated such intentions to him. Shaken, he retired to his chambers to ponder her fate—only to return and impose probation.

Dawn thought of the babies dying, vowed silently to return to Lovejoy, and left the high-ceilinged room of judgment.

She did return to Lovejoy—and shortly afterward was picked up and held for her probation violation. Dawn awaited the hearing on the matter before Judge Amiton.

She had been in jail for four grueling days waiting for that hearing. "I never really gave jail a serious thought," she realized during her first hours in the dingy light of the smoke-filled module. She ached for her family.

On the night before the hearing with Amiton, Dawn was in anguish, looking for any way out. "If four days would do this . . . ?" She dared not finish the question.

Dawn spoke on the phone with her daughters the night before the probation revocation hearing. She steeled herself for the worst—a jail sentence. Carefully, she explained to her seven- and nine-year-old daughters, "If I promise not to rescue, I'm sure the judge will let me come home." Dawn could hear the sounds of a brief whispered conference through the hand cupped over the receiver. It seemed like forever, but the elder girl returned, voice full of pumped-up bravery, "Mom, if you have to do that, you'll just have to tell the judge, 'Too bad!' "

The following morning, Dawn awoke. She prayed again for release as she tried in vain to ready herself for court time. The faded denim dress, thousand-time recycled underwear, and plastic sandals did not lend themselves to the feeling of a presentable appearance. She was led down to a holding area for miscreants. Dawn and two other rescuers with probation violations tried to straighten their hair and bring some color to their cheeks.

A room away—it may as well have been another planet—

was her family. Anxious to see them, anxious for them not to see her this way, she counted the creeping minutes.

The bailiff swung the door wide, ordering them to the hearing room. As she stepped across the threshold from the prisoner's bleak world to the rich wood-paneled universe of officialdom, she was taken aback by the courtroom packed with supporters. Mutely, she was directed to her chair. Lowering herself into the seat, she reached back for one clasp of her husband's hand. In a flurry, two bailiffs intercepted the move and forbade the simple greeting to the man who had been like a shelter to her for over ten years.

When the brief hearing was over, Amiton had given her thirty days. Doug had words for this man. He stole back into the wood-paneled, now-empty courtroom. He looked up and there was Judge Amiton, enthroned behind the bench, representing the power that had just given Dawn the maximum sentence for trespassing. There he was, ebony-robed, his gavel of authority lying on its side before him. He was leaning his head against the leather chair back, looking to the ceiling where no god dwelt—looking—his eyes filled with tears.

Doug felt the emptiness as he withdrew silently from the courtroom.

Emptiness, however, was not what Dawn felt as she was escorted back to her cell. Was it disappointment? Outrage? Anger? Shock? It was all of these. Stoically, she marched back under the watchful, suspicion-laden eyes of her captors, but in the relative privacy of her Spartan cage she spent the next hour in tears. Flinging herself on the unyielding bunk, she wasted the time in self-pity.

"I had the loudest pity party I'd ever had," Dawn admitted. But soon she realized it was no good to carry on like that. She calmed herself and turned her thoughts to the Savior she adored. The Spirit of God, now more audible to her in her content state of mind, said, "Be still and know

that I am your God! You are Mine; you are not here without
a purpose."

Cautiously, the other prisoners began to approach her.
She was an anomaly in their midst. "Sure!" they said to
themselves, "there are churches, but does *Christianity* still
exist?" They were doubtful. From then on, Dawn's time was
consumed. Self-centered pity parties were not possible. Her
every waking moment was absorbed by the black hole of
the other inmates' spiritual poverty. Penning long overdue
letters to mothers of illiterate inmates, sharing the Gospel
of Jesus Christ, and spreading the truth about the horror of
abortion comprised only a part of her newfound duties in
this shrunken world.

The days passed with blinding speed. But on a February
night, just scant minutes after midnight, Dawn heard the
words, "Stover! Roll up!" over the P.A. system. It was the
sound she had longed to hear. As she fumbled with her
belongings—the mail and the books sent by friends—she
spilled bits and pieces all over the stairs. Then she looked
back.

She had faced few sights so compelling in her life. Each
cell door with its window had a woman's face pressed
against it, some with tears in their eyes, others waving a
hand. Until then she had tried to move quietly, not wishing
to wake anyone at that early morning hour. Looking to the
center of the module where half the women slept on the
floor, she saw that they were standing and kneeling as if in a
mute salute. Guards looked on nervously because anything
done in unison by prisoners generally signaled trouble.

Never was Dawn so anxious to leave anywhere; never was
she so drawn to stay. The door crashed closed, amputating
her from these prostitutes, killers, drug users, and thieves
that she had come to love. But bars, walls, and steel doors
could never cut the ties she now had to the imprisoned.

In the waiting room, she was greeted with two of the

pleasures that had been denied her for the last month: beauty, in the form of flowers, and gum! *What a world!* Dawn thought as she rushed outside into the crisp, clear February night to breathe unrecirculated air. "What a wonderful taste!" she said.

Riding home, looking at the stars, she was dazed by her suddenly expanded universe. The awkwardness and giddiness of that sensation lingered for days.

Something else lingered—waiting patiently at the edges of consciousness. "No," Dawn resisted, "not yet. I don't want to face that yet." But she knew that it was no phantom; it was Reality, which insisted on being there. Yes, she had rescued babies—several times. Now she had been to jail for it. Was it over?

"Do I still keep rescuing?" she asked herself.

"Yes" was the answer from Reality. "Babies still die."

"How long?" Dawn persisted, but there was no answer.

At home, Dawn greedily resumed her calling as mother to her children. More than anything, she missed the home schooling of her children, making special meals, engaging with her husband in the daily joys and sorrows of making a home. Briefly, she lost herself in the warmth of the calling she most loved. There was an uneasy truce between homemaker and activist, but even Doug knew that it would not last. He knew that this was his sacrifice for the work of God, and he accepted it.

Dawn's rescues and jailing revealed her mettle, and soon national efforts like Operation Rescue called for her solid help in their campaigns. Leaders of the budding rescue movement in Seattle, Washington, called on her to help guide Washington's first statewide rescue.

Dawn arrived at the home of some local Washington activists. It was a natural wood upper-middle-class home outside Seattle. She approached through gently curving tree-lined streets on a starless September night in 1988. She never clearly saw the nearby lake or surroundings since it was still dark when she left early the next morning to stake out the rescue site.

Light eked through the overcast as they exited the highway and moved toward the medical building cluster in Renton, Washington, that surrounded the target. Indecisive clouds gave forth showers, then mists, then showers again as Dawn and the others arrived. They parked several blocks away, waiting and watching.

The dark brown Cedar River Clinic building sat nestled among the landscaped shrubbery. The bustle in and about the clinic indicated that the staff were trying to be prepared, though they could not be sure their clinic was the target. A lone police officer sat in his idling cruiser looking more bored than attentive.

Light grew during the agonizing wait, but Dawn felt excitement in her spirit. Quickly, she began directing rescuers as carload after carload arrived, eventually almost two hundred in all. Dawn rejoiced in the freedom she had to both block the heavy wooden doors and freely move about sidewalk counseling.

The mild intermittent rain did not dampen the singing, praise, and prayer of the throng of rescuers planted before the five entrances. Wet psalters and worshiping hearts were everywhere opened, filling the air with a sweet savor. The strangely silent counterdemonstrators seemed befuddled.

Police numbers grew slowly, radical women's groups gathered and gaggled across the street, and escorts sought to force gaps through the massed rescuers. Police joined escorts to try to break through where Dawn was stationed. Rescuers stood linking arms, and Dawn pleaded with police. Finally, the leading officer said, "We're not going to get in this door. It is not worth it."

Dawn immediately turned her attentions to an abortion-bound mother, calling on her to reconsider. Following the woman away from the door, she continued to plead over the shouts of the escorts. Dawn made a commitment to herself.

She could not even see the woman for the clot of escorts gathered around. "I just resolved in my heart that that child was not going to die that day."

She forged ahead, though she was leaving the relative safety of the other rescuers. The young woman suddenly broke loose of the huddle of pro-abortion escorts, saying to them, "Leave me alone! I'm leaving this place!"

As she rode back to her Hillsboro home from Seattle that night, Dawn's satisfaction over this rescue was evident. But following close on the heels of that satisfaction was the voice of Reality again.

Leaning against the glass, looking at the night lights passing, Dawn wondered, "Must I rescue again?"

Reality asked, "Are children dying out there today?"

Dawn looked at the passing lights of a small, nameless town, "Yes, even there—but how long?"

There was no answer.

JESSE LEE

Greenwich Village Minister
for Life

"Hi, my name is Mary. Do you know Jesus?"

The simple introduction surprised Jesse Lee as he stood just inside the door of the Greenwich Village storefront church. He had been invited to the Neighborhood Church by two fellow students at the acting school. Jesse had arrived early, opened the door, peered inside, and cautiously stepped in.

Mary's voice had startled Jesse, but there was more. Her question, "Do you know Jesus?" was borne by unexpected power. Jesse instinctively knew that Mary knew Jesus and that Jesus was somebody to know. Inside him, years of encrusted rebellion and callous disregard for truth began to crack. Such was the power of her words rolling over and over in his mind.

Jesse came to New York City at the peak of his rebellion against his own father—and God. The towering buildings and the driven herds of humanity in the city held no attraction for him. He intended to complete his acting education and flee back to the rural life that was embedded in his soul. But now the power of Christ held him fast and began changing his corrupt conscience.

Jesse stayed with the little Greenwich Village church and grew strong in its activist soil. There was no room for equivocation for this small church or its members since they were a lonely island of normalcy in the midst of a viv-idly debauched cult of hedonism. Places near the church tended to be family businesses, but the rest of the Village was the central cesspool of the moral corruption of New York City. The Village was littered with lesbian bars and other businesses brazenly catering to sodomite perversity. The church was always more deeply challenged to be the light Christ called it to be.

"New York is big and imposing, and it's discouraging if you don't fight it," Jesse says. "It is as though these tall buildings speak to you and say, 'You're insignificant. You can't change anything. Sin is institutionalized here. Forget it!'"

Six years after their first meeting, Mary and Jesse were married. While Jesse's conscience became more sin sensi-tive, God was preparing him to move into ministry in the eleven-and-one-half-foot wide Neighborhood Church. This was far from the pastoral scenes of rural life painted by his previous desires.

The ministry at Neighborhood Church had the reputa-tion of involvement in every aspect of life. Difficult issues were squarely faced. The perverse population of the Village was self-affirming and tough. Jesse explains, "A sodomite can live in a building that is all sodomite. He can work in a business that is all sodomite. He can go to restaurants that are virtually all sodomite. He can live in a ghetto and not have to deal with very many heterosexuals in a typical day."

Having been drawn out of the selfish and casual mind-set that is the mainstay of the abortion industry, Jesse was particularly vehement about the abortion issue. When a journalist, Richard Cowden-Guido, told Jesse about Joan Andrews and other rescuers, a measure of pride in what he had already been involved in caused Jesse to stand off. "When I heard of somebody doing something that I hadn't done yet," Jesse says, "I think I was a little uppity."

But Jesse also had other concerns. "There were a lot of crackpots involved whose motivation was not right," he explains. "Some of them didn't have a full deck to play with."

With Jesse's reluctance in mind, Cowden-Guido arranged for Jesse to meet Operation Rescue founder, Randy Terry, over the phone. He cradled the receiver and listened carefully for the markers of fanaticism. What he heard was an obedient servant of God, and his suspicions dissolved. Randy's and Jesse's strong bonds to Christ provided a seedbed for a deep-rooted friendship and trust to develop. Jesse made plans to meet Randy at the March For Life in Washington, D.C., on the anniversary of the tragic *Roe v. Wade* decision.

On that crisp January afternoon, the crowd moved toward the steps of the Supreme Court building. Jesse had lost Randy in the crushing congregation. Approaching the Greco-Roman edifice, he spotted Randy with a microphone and jury-rigged speakers. Randy paced and gestured. He cried and pleaded. Arms outstretched and hands open, Randy invoked the heroes of Scripture and showed the course of history changed for the good by willing believers. Finally, he cried, "If abortion is murder, why don't we *act* like it's murder?"

Those words went deep. In power, they were reminiscent of the words Mary had first spoken to him years earlier. As Jesse recognized the inherent truth in the words, shame washed over him.

Randy's words found solid footing on the Word of God planted in Jesse's heart. He was convinced that rescues were right before God, but one thing remained to be done. He needed to check the spiritual commitment of Randy Terry and the other Operation Rescue leaders.

Jesse visited with Randy at his Binghamton, New York, home to meet these leaders. The serious and prayerful attitude with which they approached their rescue work impressed Jesse. Confident of the godly leadership of

Operation Rescue, he joined the ranks. Confident of Jesse's abilities and heart, Randy brought him in on the planning of the historic event. Jesse's knowledge of New York City's subway maze would prove invaluable.

At Operation Rescue's kickoff on May 2, 1988, Jesse emanated the confidence that can come only from knowing God is there. "I was up for it," he says. "God had given me peace about this. I was looking forward to seeing God manifest in some way, and I wasn't disappointed."

Jesse was invigorated. The cool gray dawn arrived. In the lobby of the Times Square Hotel, a dingy remnant of an era when even cheap hotels had standards, rescuers huddled in small knots for prayer. The room rates here had suited the pocketbooks of many rescuers who had already sacrificed greatly to be in New York. "Some of these people," he remembers, "didn't even have enough money to stay at the Times Square Hotel. They slept on a floor somewhere to come to New York to do this rescue."

All gathered outside where a small band of howling pro-aborts railed from across the street. Jesse led a prayer and raised high the small American flag that marked him as an Operation Rescue guide, and he stepped quickly toward the descending stairway leading to the subway's bowels. With his contingent close behind, Jesse boarded the train leading toward the Margaret Sanger Planned Parenthood Headquarters in downtown Manhattan. Several stops later, they debarked, crossed the cement pad, and moved aboard an uptown train.

Light-blue-jacketed community relations officers accompanied the seven hundred people of Operation Rescue as they shuttled through the underground maze. Uniformed officers reported the rescuers' movements by radio. Counterdemonstrators, mingling and mocking, made raucous noises and obscene remarks to the evident distaste of both rescuers and police. Commuters surrendered brief puzzled glances at the unusually packed cars and flag-bearing guides, then dove back into a *Times* or *Newsday*.

"Operation Rescue—*off!*" Jesse called at Eighty-six Street and Lexington Avenue. The command was carried by other voices throughout the battered cars. The rescuers pushed through the exits, regrouped, and ascended the stairs to the cacophony in the street above.

"Walk quickly—no running!" reminded the crowd marshals who wore the black armband with the yellow "OR." The stream of rescuers rounded the corner heading for the Eighty-fifth Street abortuary of Herbert Schwarz.

Jesse led his band and sat at the door of the off-white nondescript brick building. Within minutes, over five hundred people were sitting worshiping and praying in the sight of the perplexed passers-by. Another two hundred pro-lifers interceded in prayer or sidewalk counseled.

Police numbers mounted slowly until there were more than 350 officers milling anxiously and trying to avoid the shrill whistles and belligerent chants of the pro-aborts: "Racist—sexist—anti-gay, born-again bigots, go away!"

They screamed incessantly while pastors led rescuers in prayer and song. "It was like a big happy church service outside in front of the abortion chamber," Jesse observed. "It was just glorious. The Spirit of God was there."

Soon police began to remove rescuers on stretchers. An audible gasp rippled through the crowd as the first nuns were arrested and carted off. Every Catholic officer could be identified by his blush.

Directing the troops by bullhorn from near the door, Randy Terry commanded the seated multitude to "skooch" over as each rescuer was arrested and fill the empty place. This allowed police to make little headway. They had hoped to clear a path to the door. Terry begged police to slow the arrests to give more time to the babies. As they were hauled away, rescuers joined in fervent prayer for the

New York City police. Crowd marshals plucked up small knots of rescuers and moved them to fill gaps created by arrests to keep the doors blocked longer. Curious passers-by gaped at the strange contest.

The clinic never opened that day.

But Jesse realized that the war had only begun in New York. Philadelphia, Atlanta, and Washington, D.C., rescues were all in the offing. Spreading the message so that rescue movements would spring to life among obedient Christians across the country was one of the goals of Operation Rescue, and Jesse took every opportunity to provoke believers to this obedience.

Jesse's help was in demand as Operation Rescue developed its strategy for its second wave in Atlanta during early October. The first wave, in July during the Democratic National Convention, had been planned as a four-day affair, but as with Christ's loaves and fishes, it had been multiplied. Some had spent forty days in the Fulton County jail. Atlanta coffers had been bled for over $500,000.

In October, Jesse's plane touched down with a muted bump in Atlanta's sprawling airport. He prayed silently as he thought forward to the Siege of Atlanta. Clouds covered Atlanta's sky just as a darkness threatened the rescue work. This time police had openly promised the "gloves off" treatment. Pain-compliance holds, police said, would force rescuers to walk. Operation Rescue leaders tried unsuccessfully to negotiate with Atlanta police.

"They were unwilling to negotiate on anything," Jesse says. "They told us, 'We're going to make you walk. We're going to use come-along holds and make you walk to the bus.'"

To counteract that, rescuers had been taught that as they came within ten feet of the police, they were to drop to their hands and knees and continue moving on all fours. This would present the least threatening approach. Police using painful tactics would have to purposely overreact.

New rescuers joined in spite of knowing the police plan.

Jesse was appointed to lead a group bound for the Femi nist Women's Health Center. Two other contingents would confront other clinics. Timing was carefully discussed so that the other clinics would be hit sequentially, drawing officers away from the SurgiCenter and leaving it sparsely defended.

When Jesse and his 125 cohorts arrived at the clinic, they stood about five deep along the heavy pipe barricades looking up the incline to the portico. The abortionists stood up there with visibly restrained expressions of anger. Behind Jesse's nervous, prayerful group was the traffic guid- ing itself—slow and gawking—around the clump. Before them, inches away, were stony-faced officers.

"My heart was pounding," Jesse remembers. "*I'm respon- sible for these people,* I thought. I looked at that barricade, I looked at the cops, and the people looked at me. I just *had* to be the first one. That's all there was to it. I got down, and I got under the barricade. A cop put his foot on my hand, and I was all right. My butterflies went away, and the peace of the Lord came over me."

Looking to his right, Jesse saw someone else coming on his belly under the barrier from behind him. When the officers moved toward the other man, Jesse inched forward again. Back and forth the officer jumped, trying to stanch the flow of rescues. Then a third person came under the barricades—a fourth—then a swarm. Jesse remembered Psalm 34:7: "The angel of the LORD encamps around those who fear him, and delivers them." As he looked at the po- liceman standing in his riot gear, holding a club, he thought of 1 Samuel 17:45: "You come to me with a sword, a spear, and a javelin; but I come to you in the name of the LORD of hosts."

"That worked a work in me so that I didn't panic. I feel like that has changed me," he says.

Arrests did not begin for some time since the police

strength had been sapped by the two rescues in other parts of Atlanta. The depleted forces were unable to hold the line as rescuers scurried on hands and knees up the stairs to the tan-colored brick box emblazoned with the Orwellian banner, "Pro-choice is pro-life." Soon the metal doors were clogged with rescuer bodies. The clinic was bathed in prayer and worship for a while. But reinforcements arrived after a time, and arrests began—with Jesse as the first victim.

By some act of grace, Jesse was spared the promised painful holds. But that only sharpened his sensitivity as he endured hearing the others' cries of agony. "There was nobody else treated as gently as me. Everyone else was treated rough in one way or another. It seemed like clergymen were handled worse than others."

Photographers and video cameramen were rigorously herded away by police.

Once rescuers were in jail, contemptuous guards denied standard treatment to the pro-life prisoners. Despite every attempt by officials to quash the religious tone of the rescuers—even while in jail—prayer and worship continued with vigor. Guards snatched one Catholic priest and tossed him into solitary confinement for offering the Mass. Preaching was prohibited.

"I think the rescue movement is prophetic," Jesse says. "There will be some sort of division in the Church because of it. I believe that God is bringing this forth."

In spite of some answering God's call, Jesse feels that the Church may continue to suffer the abuses of the legal system because it has abdicated its proper role. "I believe a particular call goes with the message of rescue. It's a trumpet call by God. I think it is to His Church. We are to be the salt of the earth, but we haven't done it and we're being trampled underfoot by men."

LINDA WOLFE

Offered an Abortion to Solve Her "Problem"

Linda stood at the sink absently washing the dishes and looking out the window on the rain-soaked landscape. Her troubles intruded on her thoughtless pursuit. Her swollen, pregnant belly rubbed against the edge of the drainboard. "What am I supposed to do?" she asked no one in particular.

Linda was married and was rearing three children. This child-in-progress was not her husband's but the result of years of applied hedonism. Unfaithfulness was only the most recent manifestation of her rebellion.

Her pregnancy bordered on six months. Linda had recently tried to take refuge in prayer, and although that was most appropriate, her sin-seared conscience was incapable of making distinctions between right and wrong. Christ's cure for that malady was still some time away.

Yesterday, January 22, 1973, was a benchmark in American history. But history, American or otherwise, was far from Linda's mind.

She heard the faint ring of the telephone in the bedroom, shut off the water, dried her hands, and scurried out of the kitchen. Linda entered the blinding, lime green-and-gold bedroom, a gaudy remnant of the sixties psychedelic fashion. She picked up the phone and cradled it on her shoulder. "Hello?" she answered.

"Hi," the voice of a close friend returned. "Hey, I think I can help you with your problem . . . you know, the pregnancy, your marriage, and all that."

"How's that?" Linda asked.

"Well, yesterday the Supreme Court legalized abortion. I know this doctor who will do them up to six months. You might just be under the wire. You could just say you lost the baby. What d'ya think?"

Linda stood immobile. The color drained from her face. *Abortion?* she thought, and the thought made her queasy. She'd had a couple of miscarriages and was fully aware that the baby was a person. Her immorality had never extended to barbarism. She could not conceive of bringing pain to anyone—animal or human. She was certain that the baby would feel unimaginable pain during an abortion.

"Linda?" her friend trespassed into her trance. "Linda? Are you all right?"

"Yeah," Linda answered uncertainly.

"Well, what about it? You're about six months. You'd have to hurry."

"No," Linda said wanly. "No, I couldn't do that."

After the call, confusion continued to embroil Linda's life for some time. A tumultuous divorce and an eventual remarriage wrought distortions in her days. But there was no confusion about her child. Linda would raise her.

In the turmoil, however, she was found by Jesus Christ. He, like the good Samaritan, treated and bandaged her wounds and placed her in caring hands for recovery.

It was a different person who listened to the pastor urging involvement in the abortion conflict—different from the pleasure-seeking Linda of more than a decade ago. The phone call from her friend was a distant memory, but her opposition to abortion had since been calcified by the Word of God.

Jail was the furthest thing from her mind when she embarked on her pro-life journey. But picketing quickly began to seem insufficient. "If that was my child," Linda, a mother of five, reasoned, "I would do more." But "more" was uncharted territory, and "more" would soon be revealed.

Her own checkered past gave compassion to Linda's work as a sidewalk counselor. She stood on the sidewalk with her literature in hand and begged women to reconsider their choice. Often she felt drawn to simply follow the mothers from the public walk where she stood into the clinic itself, but she restrained herself. Clearly, this "more" by itself was not enough for Linda.

Later, Linda sat quietly in a dingy meeting room. She was not ambivalent as she listened attentively to the speaker, a St. Louis, Missouri, rescuer who was sure of the meaning of "more." As a result of the evening's speech, a local activist group announced a plan to participate in a Spokane, Washington, rescue. They hoped that the experienced rescuers in Spokane would help set the tone for future action in Portland. Linda signed up.

In May 1986, Linda and her husband, Darrell, drove through the dry eastern Washington landscape toward her first rescue at Spokane's Deaconess Hospital. Both were apprehensive about the rescue.

The hospital increased security but was unable to stop the prayer service that happened in the building the next day. Soon police swarmed into the lobby of the massive hospital. Praying people were carried away as curious onlookers watched. By evening the TV news had informed the entire region of the hospital's abortion policy. But "more," the hospital's surgery area where abortions were done was closed for the day.

The overwhelming success of the Spokane rescue fired Linda's zeal. Her public pro-life work, however, was soon put on hold during her daughter-in-law's difficult pregnancy. Linda's zeal was focused on her granddaughter, Liberty, who was born at five and a half months gestation. This marvel of life before Linda's eyes only affirmed her commitment to the preborn. Once Liberty was stable, Linda resumed her other pro-life work.

Linda heads into battle armed with copies of a photo of tiny, premature, newborn Liberty swimming in tubes and wires. Along with this telling picture, she displays a more current picture of Liberty and a picture of a child aborted at the same age as Liberty was at birth. The powerful trio of pictures have often balked abortion-bound mothers. Escorts, in the name of "choice," snatch the damning evidence from Linda's hands and try unsuccessfully to shred the laminated prints.

Linda makes these sets by the score. Over three hundred are in the hands of arresting officers and women across America.

In October 1988, Linda arrived in the early morning at the Atlanta, Georgia, Operation Rescue headquarters. The cool drizzling morning did not dim or hide the beauty of the Atlanta skyline. The new buildings stood erect as part of the burgeoning business center. As the rescuers waited, the sputtering clouds ceased their spitting.

Already, hundreds milled in the Motel 1 parking lot. Small knots of praying people dotted the area. "I was excited that God had called so many soldiers," Linda says.

Randy Terry emerged from the motel and spoke. He warned that there might be physical pain involved in this rescue. "I knew it wasn't anything like what was going to happen to those babies," she says. "They wouldn't be allowed to kill us."

Operation Rescue leaders gathered the flock, divided the throng into three groups, gave final instructions, prayed, and sent them on their disparate ways.

Cars, trucks, and vans laden with their human cargo la-

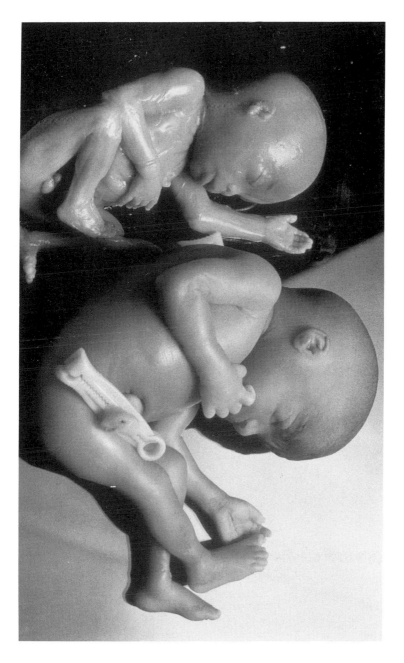

Abortions continue to occur throughout the entire nine months of pregnancy in the United States. Copyright © 1988 by Pat Cahill. All rights reserved.

Phil Tussing, standing, center of the photograph. Photo by Advocates for Life.

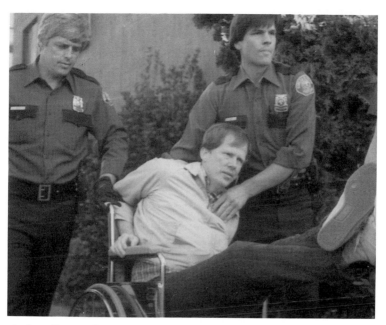

Andrew Burnett being wheeled away under arrest. Photo by Advocates for Life.

Dawn Stover is arrested for interfering with "commerce." Photo by Advocates for Life.

Under arrest, my son, Joshua deParrie, age 16. Photo by Advocates for Life.

Jeanne deParrie, handcuffed, age 13. Photo by Advocates for Life.

Judy Hager and Linda Wolfe help block an abortion clinic's entrance. Photo by Advocates for Life.

This crawl is a nonconfrontive way of stopping traffic to an abortion clinic. Copyright © 1988 by Pat Cahill. All rights reserved.

A rescue in progress. Photo by Advocates for Life.

Joan Andrews holding a niece. Photo by Advocates for Life.

Carol Armstrong (back row) and Andrew Burnett. Photo by Laura Dunn.

Rescuers turn out in Pittsburgh. Photo by Jeanne Robinson.

New York rescuers. Photo by Advocates for Life.

The hands and knees position is extremely difficult for police to control.
Copyright © 1988 Christopher Baldwin.

A *"lock 'n block"* rescue in Chicago. *The doors to the abortion clinic are locked, and two rescuers are locked to cement blocks in front. Photo by* Advocates for Life.

Kathy Stewart sidewalk counseling in Portland, Oregon. Photo by Advocates for Life.

The "come along" hold in action. Photo by Advocates for Life.

A policeman has two crawlers stopped, but the others keep going.
Copyright © 1988 Christopher Baldwin.

Jerry Falwell gives his support to nonviolent rescues. Copyright © 1988
Pat Cahill. All rights reserved.

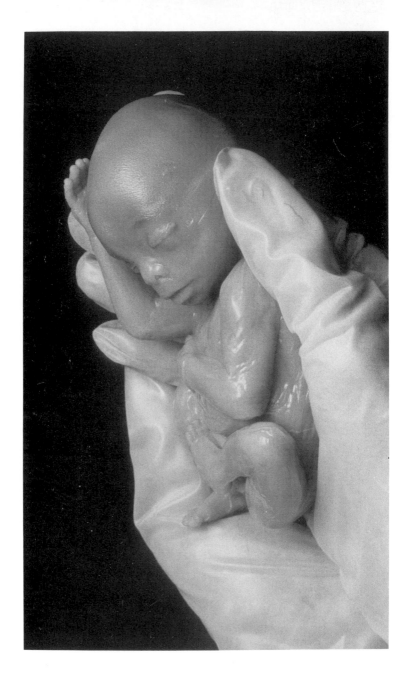

A late term aborted child, sometimes euphemistically called a "fetus."

bored off in all directions. Police were unable to snag whole groups in buses. Neither would they be able to follow the many vehicles. Linda's transport dispatched her group at the Atlanta transit train, MARTA, and they boarded the smooth, quiet tram.

After they arrived downtown, Linda's group leader led them on a diversionary walk for over an hour. They gawked like sightseers. Plainclothes police dogged their trail. At the appointed time, armed with her laminated photos, Linda marched up toward the pipe-frame barricade that blocked the street where the midtown clinic stood. Stern-faced police stood behind the barrier in riot gear. Horses, motorcycles, and police cars littered the inside of the barricaded area. As soon as the group had reached the rails, the leader saw that the sidewalks were free and led them around. When police approached, rescuers dropped to their hands and knees and continued forward.

Major Burnette of Atlanta's police force had promised "gloves off" treatment, and the police obeyed his orders. "I remember they pulled my head up," Linda says, "and took a picture. All of a sudden I was being held by my head, and all the weight was on my neck. I felt this horrible pain go through my head, and my ear hurt. I remember screaming, and then everything started seeming like it was distant.

"I remember a shocked feeling when they first grabbed me because I was at peace—praying. I felt like I was with the Lord. I remember for that second I thought, *This is what the babies feel.* They are at peace, and then someone is attacking them. It was like they said, 'We don't want you here! We don't want you, so here's what we're going to do.' And I just felt like, *That poor little baby doesn't even understand that.* I never felt so 'one' with the baby before."

Police flex-cuffed her hands behind her back and tried to force her to stand, but she was unable. "It got real black," Linda recalls. "Then I don't remember anything, except hitting my head on something. They threw me in the bus, and I hit my head on a post by the driver's seat. And they were screaming at me to get up in the seat."

Linda struggled into the seat of the white bus. She waited until the load of rescuers were driven to the processing center.

When Linda finally stumbled from the bus, she was nauseous, and her head screeched with pain. Her neck and jaw were swollen and painful, and she continued to bleed from her left ear. These symptoms persisted for four days. She feared asking for medical attention because of the experiences of others. "I wanted medical help," she explains, "but one of my friends had gone in to get medical help, and they kept her in shackles in one of those little holding cells for seven hours."

After a brief examination, the woman was declared sound and placed back in the shackles for another eight hours. Linda had no desire to partake of that treatment, but the jail's medical help was not the only help available.

"Friday, the fourth day, I was still very nauseous, and I had a bad headache and my ear was bleeding. I just went over in a little corner where nobody would go. I just wanted to pray and be alone. I told the Lord, 'I just don't think I can go much farther. I'm sick.'

"This woman came up. She's very unusual looking. She wears a long dress, a one-foot cross, and has long gray hair. She's not your run-of-the-mill person. She had a little bottle of oil, and while I was praying, she said the Lord sent me over here to anoint your ear with oil and to pray for healing. Within an hour my headache and my nausea left, and I didn't have any more bleeding."

Linda was encouraged to hear that other rescuers were being added to the ranks. She was particularly elated at the number of men willing to be arrested for the babies. "Usually, in Portland," she explains, "it has been 1 man and 12 women. This was 250 men to 100 women."

But living conditions in the women's barracks were deplorable. "There were literally thousands of cockroaches," she says, "and there was only one drinking fountain."

Rescuers were never asked their names but were assigned Baby Jane Doe numbers, which made it impossible for friends and relatives to ask about them. Linda was Baby Jane Doe #2183. During the nine-day ordeal, none of the women were given jail clothing. They were forced to live in the clothes they had on. After refusing to allow changes of clothing, officials threatened that anyone with body odor would be scrubbed by the male guards. And despite specific regulations requiring the jail to allow one hour in the exercise yard each day, rescuers were taken out only once during their imprisonment—for fifteen minutes.

The guards treated the rescuers with contempt. The barracks were jammed, but there were only nine regular prisoners in the crowd.

"They told us we were not allowed to pray," she remembers. "They told us we were not allowed to sing. While they were telling us that we were forbidden to sing, our men started singing really loud praises to the Lord. The windows were open, and the guards were running over shutting all the windows. And you could still hear them singing. We really needed that. It told us to go ahead and do it."

A priest was cast into solitary confinement for offering services for his fellow Catholics. "Also, we were not allowed to convert their prisoners. That's what they told us," she says. "We did, though. Two of them came to Jesus. It was so neat to see how the Lord really is in control of every single aspect."

After nine days, Linda was released. She immediately made her arrangements to fly home. She was anxious to be with her family again.

Poking through her purse on the plane, Linda pulled out one of her laminated picture sets. She pondered the comparison between her precious Liberty and the unfortunate aborted child. "Surely that other baby was precious to *some-one*," she wondered. "Could someone have made a difference for that child?"

ANDREW BURNETT

Making a Worthwhile Investment

It was a quiet afternoon when Andrew sat in the living room of the beach house. He propped a book in his lap and carefully scanned the words. His tall frame sank deeply into the overstuffed chair.

Through the picture window, the waves glittered in the warm afternoon sun, and the specks of fishing craft crawled by near the horizon.

Andrew's family made an annual pilgrimage to this Rockaway, Oregon, beach house. The break from the hectic affairs of his painting business gave Andrew the luxury of catching up on his reading and engaging in his favorite pastime of boating.

Andrew's eyes froze as the author quoted Matthew 6:19–21:

> Do not lay up for yourselves treasures on earth, where moth and rust consume and where thieves break in and steal, but lay up for yourselves treasures in heaven, where neither moth nor rust consumes and where thieves do not break in and steal. For where your treasure is, there will your heart be also.

It was not what the author was saying about the passage that stopped Andrew; it was the thoughts that were being poured into his mind. These thoughts questioned almost every aspect of his life. "I was really challenged to change my life style—to radically change it—and to do something for God that really counted," he says. "I thought that if we're all supposed to be storing ourselves treasures in heaven, then probably there should be a certain point of income where that's all you need to live on and beyond that point, any money that you make should be given to God.

"If people are dying around you," he remarks, "it is selfish to lavish everything on your family at the expense of people who are desperately in need. If you're off with your family and Christian friends having a good time, that's not serving God."

In contrast to the lethargy of his youth, Andrew, in recent years, had set high goals and attained them. Yet, for him, there had been something vaguely disconcerting about his business success. Now, his eyes frozen to the Scripture, he knew why. "I decided," Andrew says, "I was not really living like heaven is the thing that really matters. I had designated a certain portion—a substantial portion— of my income and given that to God. But basically I held back everything else for myself. Most of my time was spent on my family to the exclusion of desperate needs around me. It was in this whole area—money and what I did with my time—that I began to diligently seek God about what I was supposed to do."

The revelation poured in. Other Scriptures began to make more sense. A wave of shame washed over him as he leaned back and cried out to his Savior.

Later, Andrew and his father walked the sandy ribbon of beach. They watched the waves become a gushing skim spreading across the flats and quickly retreating. Andrew began to share his experience. He explained that beyond raising his children, he wanted to do something that really counted for God so that they would have a good example. "All I was teaching them," Andrew says, "was to have a good time with their kids. That really wasn't teaching them to serve God."

Upon returning to his Portland, Oregon, home, Andrew began to divest himself of life's excess baggage and search for where God would have him invest himself. Over the next year, world hunger and abortion loomed in his mind as the areas of most dire need. At work, he and a fellow painter spent many hours sorting through the abortion issue. It was still just an "issue" with them. Their combined ignorance gave them no thrust for action.

Late one night, Andrew leaned back in his chair to watch "Christian Voice," a Christian TV program. Social issues were the focus that night, but they dwelt on abortion during most of the broadcast. It was his first exposure to pro-life material. Andrew's innocence and ignorance of the surgical holocaust were shattered by the lurid pictures of murdered children and the graphic descriptions of the torturous methods of the abortionist. A chill crept up his back as the visual comparisons of the live unborn and their mutilated counterparts assaulted his eyes. Tears flowed freely—and still more freely when he realized his impotence against the slaughter. Andrew had no idea what to do.

World hunger, as an issue, was eclipsed. He thought, *There may be hungry people across the ocean, but right here in my own city babies are dying.*

Andrew had heard that Lynn Ludwick from his alma mater, Multnomah School of the Bible, was involved against abortion, so he immediately made an appointment to see her. "Lynn," he asked, "I've got a tremendous burden to try to stop abortion. What can I do?"

Ludwick recommended that he go to a clinic and begin picketing. To Andrew, this was a foreign idea. He had never been remotely connected with any kind of activism. Standing outside the Lovejoy Clinic on several successive Saturdays froze his blood. The building seemed to grow to impressive stature as he considered a lonely vigil as the sole picket. *I'd look like a nut,* he thought. So he searched for others to go with him.

An attempt to stir action in his church showed early promise but fizzled. Not to be deterred, Andrew sought to find collaborators from other sources. Twice, Andrew's nervously attempted pickets shorted out. Finally, he was able to gather a half-dozen others who marched on the clinic.

Andrew had been aghast to find that the clinic killed over one hundred defenseless children a week. He reasoned, "This child in the womb is still my neighbor, and you are supposed to love your neighbor as yourself. You should love your neighbor's children as you love yourself, even if your neighbor doesn't love his own children."

Weekly picketing was soon established, but Andrew listened with displeasure to the stream of invectives hurled by anti-abortion protesters at clinic workers and the hapless abortion-bound mothers. Yet he felt powerless to change it.

No one acquainted with Andrew's quiet demeanor would have suspected that he could lead a public and vocal advocacy. But soon Advocates for Life, with Andrew as founder and director, became the focus of pro-life activism in Portland.

In April of 1985, with a twinge of excitement, Andrew boarded a plane to Appleton, Michigan, for the first national Pro-Life Action Network (PLAN) convention. Andrew's heart leaped as he listened to the soft-spoken St. Louis activist, John Ryan, share about the peaceful, prayerful, nonviolent Missouri rescue missions. Andrew did not exhaust his questions until the first lightening of the sky the following morning. He was invigorated with conviction. "I knew this was right," he says. "What these people were doing was the best thing to do. No question about it."

But the cold reality of putting it into practice settled in as the wheels of his plane gave their protesting screech on touchdown on Portland's rain-dampened runway. Andrew sought escape from the unpleasant prospect of perhaps being the only pro-lifer willing to risk arrest. "I wanted to do rescues," Andrew admits, "but I didn't have the courage to do them."

Meanwhile, Andrew substituted sacrifice for obedience by investing heavily in a crisis pregnancy center. But God would not allow him to rest in this feigned obedience. The struggle went on for nearly a year.

Andrew devised dodges and exuded excuses. "I had come up with a hundred reasons why rescues were not necessary. So I've heard all the excuses. I made most of them up."

In the year's-end issue of *Oregon Magazine* in 1985, less than a year after the emergence of Advocates for Life, Andrew was listed among "People to Watch in '86." And, indeed, 1986 was a crucial year for the tall, shy Burnett.

In 1986 the PLAN convention was held in St. Louis, a seething pot of rescue activity. When Andrew flew in on that spring morning, his defenses against rescue were formidable. When a lone fellow activist from Portland volunteered for rescue duty, however, Andrew felt compelled to accompany her.

Lowering clouds strained the morning light of the following day. Andrew gathered his courage and mingled with 106 rescuers in a deserted parking lot two blocks from the Regency Park clinic. Fear seized him as he walked toward the dozens of squad cars with lights stabbing his eyes. "This was the first time I had ever confronted police—on anything," Andrew says.

The uniformed officers swarmed all around. A small contingent stood resolutely before the clinic doors. Others, about seventy-five feet in front of the clinic, sought futilely to halt the human tide of what was then the largest rescue mission in the world. Overwhelmed, police fell to random arrests. Andrew and others gained the door. A peace settled over him.

The vision of the small, flat-roofed box at Regency Park

awash with a sea of rescuers was inspiring, but arrests went quickly. It looked as though the clinic might open in spite of the rescue.

Inside the battered paddy wagon, Andrew looked out on the rapidly dwindling congregation. The peace he had experienced while sitting at the door evaporated. It all seemed fruitless. "What good have we done?" he asked himself as the flex-cuffs dug into his wrists. He carried this discouragement until the evening meeting where sidewalk counselors reported mothers were changing their minds. The clinic had opened—but only symbolically.

Andrew returned to the Rose City convinced. God had won the struggle with him over rescues at the 1986 PLAN convention, and Andrew would carry its volatile seed back to the emerald hills of Portland.

But Andrew was to refine the concept of peaceful, nonviolent rescue and tout the new form to the rest of the movement. A chance meeting with Joan Binninger of Portland's Planned Parenthood sharpened his focus on the needed changes. Binninger's and Burnett's paths met briefly in the darkened lobby of a Portland radio station where she had been a guest speaker. Her eyes flashed as she bitterly complained to Burnett of the emotional and verbal abuse suffered by women at the hands of picketers.

"Well, I don't do that," Andrew responded.

"But you're responsible," Binninger remarked sharply. "You got those people out there."

Andrew was stunned. Her point drove deeply into his heart, reactivating his misgivings about picketers' behavior. He had abdicated his leadership responsibility to the random self-direction of individual marchers. God had used his opponent to cast a glaring light on this inadequacy. Andrew could see that chanting, name-calling, or anything that had a combative appearance would subvert the efficacy of the rescue movement.

"Show me a group of people chanting who don't sound

angry," he says. "If I was going to be putting together any kind of demonstration or rescue, I was responsible to the community—and to the people who were coming—to do everything that I could do to make it nonviolent."

Before any rescue was done by Advocators for Life, Andrew would first try to banish all the rancor from their activities and replace it with prayer and worship. This radical change in tenor came in time for Advocates' first rescue. Even those not rescuing were charged to focus on the compelling acts of prayer and sidewalk counseling.

The rescue, small by any account, took the abortion dealers aback. Alene Klass, administrator of the Lovejoy Clinic, virtually vibrated before the TV cameras. She shook as she called it a "terrorist action," though the dozen rescuers merely sat in the procedure room singing hymns. Klass maintained that rescuers were being trained in terrorist training camps.

Looking like a big farmboy, Andrew shrugged, grinned, and admitted that rescuers could be called terrorists—*but only by scriptural definition.* "When justice is done," he quoted, "it brings joy to the righteous but terror to evildoers" (Proverbs 21:15 NIV).

Advocates began staging rescues every other month, sometimes with as few as three or four stalwarts. Pro-aborts dogged Andrew's footsteps. A controversy arose in Portland's Christian community over breaking the law.

Without warning, to the clicking of cameras and the scrawling of notes, The Saltshakers, a self-proclaimed "evangelical think-tank," announced opposition to rescues. The National Abortion Rights Action League (NARAL) commended the group. The pro-life movement in the area seemed to wane. But it sprang back when Andrew was jailed for thirty days—a maximum sentence—in a jail so overcrowded that violent criminals were routinely released to avoid exceeding occupancy guidelines. With renewed vigor, the local pro-life community rallied to the cause.

Jail did nothing to dissuade Andrew, either. Each rescue brought new lessons for him in avoiding the appearance of evil. "I was seeing that the media were picking up on the noise and the confrontation," he remembers, "and that wasn't what we were trying to promote."

Andrew's pioneering of peaceful and prayerful tactics brought national notice. So when Randy Terry, founder of Operation Rescue, first began to seriously gather forces for the bold plan, Andrew was naturally included. By that time Andrew had concluded that picket signs at a rescue were too combative for the harmlessness they wished to portray. This premise received the support of Operation Rescue leaders.

Due to large-scale efforts like Operation Rescue, this means of saving mothers and children from abortion has grown geometrically. By six months after the New York action (in which 1,646 arrests were made), there had been over 9,000 arrests across the U.S. for rescue activities. In some cases, as with the 53 who blocked a clinic in Portland, Oregon, no arrests were attempted.

Charges have been levied by the pro-abortion forces that rescuers are wrongfully hijacking the civil rights movement. But Andrew denies that the rescue movement can easily be compared to protests on other issues. He underscores the primary difference between rescues and the civil rights movements of the past. "The civil rights movement, the anti-war movement, and the people who were pushing those movements are the victims of a particular abuse," he explains. "In the case of civil rights, the primary people who were out demonstrating were black people. It was *their* civil rights they were standing up for. That's not the case with unborn children. I have never been the victim of an abortion. But these children need someone to speak for them, and I have an obligation to do something for someone else."

JULI LOESCH

Left-wing Activist Turned Pro-lifer

"If you are so concerned about what plutonium does to a baby's arm buds, you should see what a suction abortion machine does to the entire body," the woman said evenly.

Juli stood momentarily still trying to negotiate the sudden turn in subject. "Well, I'm not here to talk about abortion," Juli replied, not seeing the relevance. "I don't think it's possible for anyone to say what is right or wrong for another person. Everyone has to make up their own minds and make their own decisions."

Here she was, at what she described as an "atomic Tupperware party." Juli was speaking about the effects of radiation, specifically on the unborn, but this woman wanted to talk about abortion.

The troublesome woman persisted.

"But," she replied, "you've been trying to tell us that it is morally wrong—that it is a crime and a sin—for the military, for instance, to injure these kids accidentally. Don't you think it's wrong to kill them deliberately?"

Rolling her eyes heavenward and thinking that she was dealing with a single-issue fanatic, Juli answered, "These are two completely different things—two separate issues. Nuclear weaponry means corporations and government, a big social issue. But abortion is personal, too personal and too private."

Again the irritating woman pressed forward, "I don't think it matters whether the poison that was involved is a radioisotope or a saline solution. Poisons are poisons. Kids are kids, and dead is dead."

Juli had no answer. She had spent hours poring over embryology texts to prepare her anti-nuclear presentations. That study had unwittingly prepared her to also see the validity of the persistent woman's assertion. But she couldn't instantly admit that she'd been wrong about abortion. That 1977 home gathering proved to be a key in her turning from a self-described "ambivalent pro-choice liberal" to an organizer of direct action against abortion.

■ ■ ■

As a child, Juli had listened intently to the Gospels being read in church. The more she listened, the more she became convinced that nonviolence—putting down the sword and taking up the Cross—was the way of the Lord Jesus. Her first memory of seeing the need for direct action on the behalf of others was when she was about eight. She stared frozen at the civil rights pamphlet. The pictures jumped out, but her eyes were riveted to the text that described segregation as "tearing the Body of Christ apart." The pamphlet's vivid depiction found fertile soil in Juli's young mind. She ran up to her mother crying, "Someone's tearing the Body of Christ apart!"

Before Juli was old enough to vote, she trudged door-to-door on a voter registration drive in a black neighborhood near her home in Erie, Pennsylvania. One issue piled on another as she grew older, and soon she was involved in a whole range of environmental, nuclear, peace, and nonviolence causes.

Progressive politics, however, also led her into the kind

of sexual experimentation so common among activists of the Left in the late sixties and early seventies. She drifted away from the Church and "read" her way into a feminist social ideology. To her, abortion only vaguely resembled violence, and she actively suppressed even *that* notion. *Roe v. Wade* passed virtually unnoticed, and Juli kept her focus narrowly on nuclear issues.

But after her confrontation with the irrefutable logic of the woman at the "atomic Tupperware party," her excuses began to crumble. "Yes," she conceded, "abortion is violence," but she felt she was incompatible with the political ideology of the pro-life groups.

Wanting to resolve her ambivalence one way or the other, Juli very quietly attended a pro-life film. There she was invited to join a Shield of Roses group who were going to pray in front of an abortion clinic. Juli decided to do this rather than get involved in the political end of things. *Prayer, at least, wouldn't do any harm,* she thought as she suspiciously eyed the staid matrons in the prayer circle.

These people at this event are nicer, more intelligent, and more caring than I ever expected, Juli admitted to herself. But she still was unable to negotiate a quick and easy conversion to pro-life. She remained under the impression that pro-lifers did not care about civil rights—did not care about nonviolence—did not care about people who were already born or about anyone except those in their narrow issue.

"You know the joke," she says. "It's a stereotype that anti-abortion people are not 'the pro-life movement' but 'the pre-life movement' because they are people who believe that life begins at conception and ends at birth."

But even when she overcame her prejudices about pro-lifers, Juli still had deep concerns about the back alley abortions that might follow any reversal of the pro-abortion laws. She remembered a student nurse at a local hospital who discovered her pregnancy and shot herself in the abdomen. The woman survived, but her body was really messed up. Later Juli looked clearly at the facts of the case and realized with a start that it was clearly not an attempt at self-abortion—but attempted suicide. The graphic image of the woman bleeding on the floor held her in a spell.

Eventually, her concern for the health of the pregnant woman brought her around to an anti-abortion position. Juli was illuminated by the facts presented by Dr. Bernard Nathanson regarding the dangers of the abortion procedure, even under the best of conditions. Studies were showing that more women were dying and being physically damaged from legal abortions than prior to *Roe v. Wade*. Her gnawing fear of illegal abortion was replaced with a dread of legal abortion. "I realized that I didn't have to say, 'Choose for the baby and choose against the woman,'" Juli explains. "In fact what was good for the baby was good for the woman, too."

All this time Juli was being drawn inexorably into the pro-life movement. And the very Power that worked on her understanding of abortion seemed to be leading her to a rebirth of faith. As she began to feel the brutality toward the unborn child and sense the horror of the deliberate national slaughter, she looked around and asked, "Who is it that has been so humane and enlightened and consistent that they have realized this from the beginning?"

Juli saw that this was the Catholic church. For all its problems, the church had stressed care for mothers and children and upheld other standards of humane treatment through the centuries.

Juli's involvement in rescues followed quite naturally from her activities in civil rights. "I never had an idolatrous respect for law," she explains. "I never thought that law was the most important thing. I got involved in rescues because someone gave me a leaflet. I was at the March For Life in 1978. They gave me this leaflet, and I read it. It said that in solidarity with the women and the children, we should go to the place where they are at risk, and I thought that made sense."

Some of her left-wing feminist friends reacted. "I could tell you some pretty colorful rejection stories," she says.

But having been a mainstream feminist—and one who might easily have been panicked into an abortion—Juli understands what drives the pro-abortion sentiment. "Your reason for being pro-abortion is good," she explains. "It's your conclusion that's wrong because abortion is so disastrously bad for women. The whole abortion industry is based on capitalizing on a woman's moment of crisis and profiting from a woman's pain. I wouldn't want to change the idealism, so to speak, of the pro-abortion person in the sense that their idealism is directed toward the well-being of women. I would like to demonstrate that a society that would allow the insides of women to be torn, scraped, and violated by the millions is not a pro-woman society."

But Juli insists that there are many closet supporters on the left side of the political spectrum. Often, however, the only communication is four or five unkind words from opposite sides of the picket line. Because of this, she formed a group called Pro-Lifers for Survival. The name was important because she was targeting an anti-nuclear group known as Mobilization for Survival with all of its adjuncts, Physicians for Survival, Teachers for Survival, and others.

When Juli and her tiny group arrived and set up a table at the Mobilization for Survival conference, suddenly there was open warfare. The conference was alive with controversy. Adversaries came up and angrily scattered the pro-life literature. Vicious epithets were hurled at the mute Pro-Lifers for Survival. The controversy came to a boil.

Finally, to Juli's amazement, someone not associated with their group stepped forward into the tumultuous forum and offered a resolution that pro-lifers be welcome in Mobilization for Survival—but without the group's adopting a pro-life position. Things exploded, accusations flew, counterproposals were called out, and Juli and her group left the conference. The biggest surprise was that, even in Juli's absence—and with vehement opposition—the original resolution was passed.

Juli remains convinced that there is an untapped reserve of pro-life support on the political Left. It simply needs to be properly confronted and cultivated.

"It is not important to care about 'the pro-life movement' or 'the abortion issue,'" she says. "Care about one child, one woman, one man, one family, one potential family that's being hurt. Go to one clinic. Try to talk to one woman. If you can personalize it, if you can make it as individual as possible, whatever you do will be real. It will be based on a real loyalty to a real person. And it will be much more worthwhile in the long run than some abstract thing you do because the 'idea' of abortion is intellectually abhorrent to you.

"I think you can make serious mistakes by forgetting that these babies are dying one by one—one by one! So I would really urge people to go to the clinic once, that's the place where the babies are killed, and talk to one woman and experience both the frustration and the sense of urgency you'll get as you realize, 'My God! Save them! They're slipping through our hands!'"

DAVE PACKER

A Policeman Who Refused Guard Duty

The orderly carried the pathological waste down the dark stairwell toward the hospital incinerator. Suddenly, the bag moved. In terror, he threw the bag into the open maw of the inferno.

It did not occur to the orderly until afterward that the "pathological waste" was a child. A professor at the hospital was conducting gruesome experiments on how late in a pregnancy he could do a prostaglandin abortion. Some resulted in the ultimate complication—a live birth. The child the orderly carried had been the pathetic victim of the macabre "experiment."

Dave Packer cringed as the orderly described the horrifying tale. He was already uneasy with abortion. His own duties often led to his working in the operating theater where abortions were performed.

Abortion had long been legal in England—a pedestrian occurrence. But nothing in the slow-paced, rural upbringing in Worminghall, England, had prepared him for the casual brutality.

Here at Churchill Hospital, Dave met his future bride, Anne. She was a nurse. One morning, in the course of her duties, she walked into a sluice room and flicked on the light. Suddenly revealed in the light were the bodies of dozens of aborted babies. "My mouth fell open, my eyes filled with tears, and the hair on the back of my neck stood up," she says.

That was the day she joined the pro-life movement.

By the time they married in 1974, their combined horror stories cinched their convictions on abortion. Their time at the hospital had imprinted them with the unspeakable carnage. "The obvious thing was," he remembers, "we were talking about *babies*—not about 'conceptuses' and lumps of God-knows-what people try and make us believe are being expelled from the womb."

The clinic owned by Henry Morganthaler was one of a chain of abortion clinics, which were glaring exceptions in Canada. Canadian law prohibited free-standing abortion clinics. The Harbord Street Morganthaler Clinic was clearly beyond the pale.

Although there was no actual evidence of a threat to the clinic, the Toronto, Ontario, police had established a twenty-four-hour guard on the unlawful clinic—seven days a week. No special instructions were given to the guards, such as one might expect for a watch against "terrorists."

Dave was now a constable in Toronto. Fourteen years had passed since his marriage to Anne in England. It sickened him to see this abuse of police resources, especially for an abortion clinic. "We were sitting there in uniform," Dave explains. "We were symbols of law and order and, by our presence, saying that this place is a legitimate organization worthy of police protection."

As a member of two pro-life organizations, Packer was appalled at the prospect of such duty. But early in the history of the Morganthaler private police guard, Constable Packer was called in as a last-minute replacement. Dave stiffened, but he went. In the ensuing months, he was assigned abortion clinic duty at night on three other occasions.

At first, he justified his actions, saying that the killing took place only during the day. Dave could see the damage caused by the mere symbolism of the law guarding that clinic, but he was still unwilling to refuse the duty. "I had all the big convictions," he says, "but whether it was to see how it would go or because I was suddenly thrust there—or for less charitable reasons—I *did* sit there. And it was an absolutely hellish experience—realizing how close I was and how implicated I was."

The contradiction ate at Dave's soul. Even his limited calls to this duty were profoundly bothering his conscience.

So on April 8, 1987, Dave privately approached his superior and told him he must refuse guard duty at the clinic. The response was an impassive, "Oh, well then, I'd better see the boss about this."

Immediately, Packer was taken off the streets and tucked away in an office sorting papers pending the necessary hearings. But on January 26, 1988, the Toronto, Ontario, Police Department formally fired Constable Packer for insubordination. The papers had been abuzz with his story. Opinions, pro and con, ran in the editorial pages. But the firing ignited interest anew. Packer found himself at the vortex of controversy.

Public attention was the furthest thing from his mind when this began. Solitude is a more likely companion for him. "I feel I was born to laze away the day trying to work out how to bring a chub out of a river," Packer has said. But instead, the press's coverage of the department's expulsion has thrust him into the limelight, apparently making his a popular cause.

Dave enjoys the support of the rank-and-file officers, but the ironclad hierarchy has turned its cold, belligerent aim toward him. Two years ago, this same police department cited Constable Packer for bravery. He had rushed into a burning high-rise and saved a three-month-old child and his mother. Now Dave was sacked for taking a stand to protect children just a few months younger.

Most of Dave's friends were stunned by the arbitrary prosecution. Even an open appeal from Mother Teresa of Calcutta was stonily rejected by the commanding officers. The harsh sentence has drawn fellow officers even closer to his side. They realize that he has been punished without just cause. It astonishes them that his mere exercise of conscience has brought such a virulent response after ten years of unblemished service. They worry that they might be subject to unjust firing as well.

But another nail has been driven into Canada's coffin. The day following Packer's firing, the Canadian Supreme Court struck down all the nation's abortion regulations, catching Canadian pro-lifers flat-footed. In a decision that mirrors the U.S.'s *Roe v. Wade* decision, they stripped the unborn of all protection. The act also legalized Morganthaler's clinics, including the one that Constable Packer refused to guard.

"I think it's important to tell pro-lifers in Canada," Dave comments, "that we have been morally 'nuked' by this equivalent of *Roe v. Wade*. Our society, which—until now— has merely been walking down the wrong path, has broken into quite a run.

"The U.S. Supreme Court looks absolutely asinine in its 1857 decision on Dred Scott, making him into a thing and not a person. This decision by the Canadian Supreme Court will look equally asinine in the history books."

Packer does not see himself as particularly courageous. "I must tell you," he admits, "that for the longest time I did nothing while I knew of the slaughter of my unborn brothers and sisters. 'The worm has turned' would probably be a better way of describing what I did.

"Rest assured, though, that after such a slow start, this is my life's work. I would urge you to tell any police officer you meet who is having trouble squaring this horror with himself that the night before my refusal to obey was very restless. But when the time came, it was the easiest and most natural thing I have ever done. I have not regretted it at all and am at peace with myself."

Dave had been taught from his youth, "Any man, who *is* a man, should stand up for what he believes is right."

The appeal on his firing has yet to reach its top level. The department strains under the requirement to keep Dave on until the last appeal is exhausted. But Dave sees that, barring a miracle, his case will be lost and his career finished.

There is no self-pity in his words. Dave says, "My situation is exactly the same as that of police officers in the U.S. To be against abortion in private would be the safe thing to do. But a man cannot stay silent while the most massive holocaust this planet has ever known is going on day after day.

"I told the chief of police here, by finding me guilty, he is simply finding himself guilty. I fully believe that I will live to see the day when new Nuremberg trials will be convened, and it will be his turn in the prisoner box."

BOB LEWIS

Committed to the Sanctity of Human Life

The pregnant young woman and her boyfriend stood at Pastor Bob Lewis's office door. They were there for counseling.

Weeks earlier the woman had walked past sidewalk counselors, past Lewis and his picket sign, and into the clinic. While she waited for her abortion, rescuers had come into the waiting room. Some began to plead with mothers for the lives of their children; others sang hymns and prayed. Suddenly, the woman knew she was in the wrong place. In the confusion, the clinic staff scurrying to empty the room, she left.

Was it only coincidence that brought this same mother to Bob Lewis's office for counsel? Bob thought not. Her appearance had been the exclamation point on his answer from Scripture about rescuing. "That act on her part," Bob says, "and the fact that there was a baby rescued as a result of that rescue effort by our pro-life people around here really showed me that it does work. Rescue does work! We may see only one or two, but they're one or two that are alive."

On the following Good Friday, Pastor Bob Lewis exited from the same clinic as the young woman. But Lewis was airborne when he left. Two police officers tossed him onto a heap of rescuers below the front porch of the clinic.

94

It had taken fifty years for God to bring Pastor Lewis to this unceremonious end.

■ ■ ■

His early home life was difficult for the first twelve years. The reek of alcohol and the physical abuse from both parents hardened Bob. But when his father died, things went straight downhill. His two sisters suffered the worst of their mother's abuse. In an awkward child's attempt to draw attention to his two sisters' plight, he ran away from home. His subsequent capture led only to his spending a couple of months in a county workhouse in Salt Lake City. He was extradited back to Minnesota and placed on probation.

The first ray of hope came from his probation officer. The man was observant enough to see Bob's bitterness over the treatment of his sisters. The probation officer also noticed Bob drifting back to other troubled kids, so he offered Bob a deal. If Bob would agree to go to a church-run farm for delinquent boys, he would make sure that his sisters were taken from their mother. So Bob and his brother moved in with a family on a western Minnesota farm.

The hard work and simple life at the farm quelled his rancor. Open skies and fresh air seemed to sedate the angry drive in Bob. During his stay on that farm, he first met Jesus Christ as Savior and Lord. For several years he grew in grace. But after his transfer to another farm in his sophomore year of high school, Bob began to drift from God.

Lewis did well academically in high school, and after graduation, he began to attend the University of Minnesota. His slow drift widened the gap in his fellowship with the Lord. After the first quarter at college, he was frustrated. He couldn't find anything he could give his life to. On campus that fall, Bob felt an abiding urge to discover his place in this life. Many Korean veterans who were attending there recommended that Bob enlist in the service

and pick up the G.I. Bill for future education. He felt this
was sound advice, so he quit school and joined the Marine
Corps.

In the Marines, Bob was selected for the very first class of
the Air Force Academy. He was briefly disappointed when
he was disqualified because of a broken nose, but the Naval
Flight School was not so worried about broken noses. It
readily accepted Bob.

It was in 1958 that Bob met and married Janice. Over
the next several years, he went from flight instructor to
fighter pilot. His record led to his selection to fly reconnais-
sance in Asia and against Castro during the Cuban block-
ade.

In the early sixties Bob began to return to fellowship
with Christ. After several years, he realized that he wanted
to make a better contribution to the Gospel—as a mission-
ary or a pastor. So with his wife and three children, he left
the military behind in 1966. Subsequently, he became involved with The Navigators ministry, joining their staff and
continuing with them for the next seventeen years.

His upbringing in foster care had given him a heart for
young people, especially those who were in need of someplace to belong. He could feel the emptiness and alienation
that haunted these children. Over the years with The Navigators, Bob and Janice have taken over a hundred young
people into their home for various reasons and various
lengths of time. More than a score were foster children.

Foster children were visible to Bob. They could be
helped individually. But those who were dying in abortion
clinics were unseen. In a Texas apartment complex, Bob
was to have his first face-off with abortion. At the time, he
and his wife were overseers for a girls' apartment complex
for The Navigators ministry.

When some of the women from the apartments first approached Bob and Janice, they were fighting tears. They
choked up as they told of the unbearable pressure on them

as nurses to assist in abortions. *Roe v. Wade* loomed only months away, but the hospital had already loosened the criteria for obtaining abortions. The women looked waxen as they described having to carry dead babies in plastic bags to a disposal area. *This can't be happening,* Bob thought. But he said, "It is murder. You have to refuse."

This episode deeply disturbed Lewis, but he didn't know what to do about it. As early as the 1973 *Roe v. Wade* decision, he sought ways to reach out to help by making contributions, writing letters, and going to meetings. Arguments for picketing and other kinds of activism soon reached his ears, but he was unconvinced, especially in the area of breaking the law. But one of Bob's assistants was attending Westminster Seminary, and a number of seminarians were getting involved in direct action. This assistant was carrying their arguments to Pastor Lewis, and he played "devil's advocate."

In 1984 these students went on their first rescue. When a politician friend of Bob's endorsed their actions, he was forced to give it more serious thought. As he continued to ponder the issue of rescues, he also began picketing the local abortion clinic.

"I continued my wrestling with the issue of the Scriptures," Bob says, "and the more I wrestled with it, the more I realized that I had a greater responsibility than just picketing. I had a moral obligation to seek to rescue the young child going into the abortion chamber in the womb of its mother.

"During all that time, I had wrestled with all the pro-life issues but never had considered it from the perspective of the infant. It was always the perspective of the mother. My argument would have been, 'Because the state doesn't command her to have an abortion, there's nothing I can do. She goes in of her own choice.' But I had never thought of that poor little infant."

Bob adds, "I had memorized all kinds of passages of

Scripture that would really touch on that . . . Proverbs 31:8–9, Proverbs 24:11–12 . . . scads of passages. All of a sudden those passages of Scripture began to come home with increasing force in my mind.

"The Scriptures say, 'Render to Caesar the things that are Caesar's, and to God the things that are God's.' It is not Caesar's right to permit the killing of the innocent; it does not fall within his purview.

"When Caesar begins to make laws that either prohibit me from obeying God or prohibit me from fulfilling the commands of God in terms of 'doing good,' he transgresses his rightful authority. And in this case the Bible commands me to do good. Surely the attempt to save the life of an innocent person is good in a biblical sense."

And so it was on Good Friday of 1986 that Pastor Bob Lewis passed the astonished escorts and walked into the waiting room of an abortion clinic. He was bent on counseling. The Word of God had fully convinced him that he must participate, and the pregnant young woman who had come to him for counseling showed it was effective. Bob had been one of those who was picketing the day she went to the clinic. Picketing and counseling had not stopped her; the rescue had.

Since that Good Friday, Pastor Lewis has been involved in many other rescues. He firmly believes that this work is not only effective but biblically mandated. "As I thought about it," he says, "the issue I had to arrive at was not, 'Was it pragmatically effective?' The first thing I had to establish in my mind was, 'Was it biblically justifiable?' Because whether or not it is ever effective is not the issue. It is, 'What does God say should be done?' and do that!

"The first thing I would encourage Christians to do is to consider the issue from the perspective of the innocent third party, from the perspective of that little child in there. And then ask them, 'If you say that is an infant with value in the sight of God—it's alive—it's a person—it's a worthy individual,' why doesn't it merit some sort of response on your part, more than just writing a letter? Why don't you periodically place yourself in the path of that abortionist and that mother and try to rescue that little one?

"If we Christians are committed to the sanctity of human life and say that what is going on in there is murder, then we ought to act correspondingly. Or at least in the terms of some moral honesty, stop using the word *murder*.

"The longer we wait, the harder it is to do something."

JUDY HAGER

Homemaker for Life

Judy looked out the plate glass window of her hillside home. She had heard the laboring motor of the school bus. Knowing what was next, she partook of the ritual of meeting. She watched her son, Christian, jump—all arms, legs, lunch box, and coat—out of the rattling doors of the brilliant yellow vehicle.

Christian bolted for the front door, negotiating the turn just inside the house. The eight-year-old boy ran to his mother.

Judy could see the concern cloud his face as he came toward her. Her sunny-faced towhead seemed overshadowed in a darkened world of turmoil. "Mom," he asked earnestly, "is it true that moms can kill their babies if they don't want them?"

Judy questioned him, "Why do you ask?" Christian said that some bigger boys had told him that if his mother hadn't wanted him, she could have killed him. Judy sought to comfort Christian by saying that she had wanted him then—and still wanted him. But he persisted, wanting to know if it was true that mothers could kill their children before they were born. Finally, she was forced to confirm the truth.

She stood there shaken to the core of her being. It was

the first time that *she* had faced the issue so squarely. Christian was oblivious to having shattered her self-protective shell and wandered off to play.

Until that day, Judy's only contact with abortion had been the late-night calls she received from a tortured friend who had gotten one years earlier. Every year on the anniversary of *Roe v. Wade*, the airwaves were packed cathode tube to silicon chip with the subject. Judy's phone would ring. From the receiver would come the anguished voice of a woman with empty arms. Other than that, Judy had successfully avoided the painful subject.

But the day she collided with abortion because of her son's question, Judy struggled out of her timid persona and contacted the only pro-life organization she knew. She volunteered at Right to Life. Judy had had longstanding bouts with depression, and these began to abate on the day she began to volunteer. God began to open her eyes to the suffering of *others*, and she started to obey His call.

During the first few times at the RTL office, she overheard discussions about the leader of another local pro-life group. When she heard him referred to as a "fanatic," her attention was piqued. She had long had an affinity with those called "fanatic." During her school days, she had been called that same name because of her dogged grip on Christian standards.

She set out to contact him, and soon she was involved in pickets and many other activities with his group. But she quickly discovered that this man was no fanatic at all. He simply acted decisively on his faith in Jesus Christ. He was a real Christian . . . an activist.

After a trip to St. Louis, this activist, Andrew Burnett, became convinced that rescue missions were necessary to save more babies. "After all our picketing, letter writing, sidewalk counseling, and crisis pregnancy work," he said, "one and a half million babies a year still get by us and die."

She knew he was right. She knew God wanted her to do

it, but *she* didn't want to. Consequently, Judy vanished from pro-life work. She continued her support of that ministry, but she did so from afar. She tried to fill that void by beginning new family activities and working at a center for handicapped children. She spent a self-serving year running, Jonah-like, from what she knew was her calling.

Judy's conscience would not rest. She tried to bargain with God. She agreed to picket, sidewalk counsel, do office work—anything pro-life—except rescue. Just as she strove with God, she received a call asking if she would help assemble and mail the pro-life newsletter. She instantly agreed. While she was there, Burnett asked her, quite simply, if she would be interested in joining the next rescue mission. She replied, "Yes." Puzzled as to why she had done that, Judy pushed it to the back of her mind. *I can always excuse myself later,* she thought, but a good excuse never arose. Instead, God broke down her disobedience. By the time she entered the clinic on that cool morning, she was at peace with God.

Judy paced in the windowless ladies' room on the fourth floor of the tall glass-in medical complex. She and four others had separately stolen in to the building when the main doors were first opened. Each by a different route, they attained the bleak restrooms—and waited—and prayed.

Andrew signaled the women from outside the door. They all scurried down the hall. One rescuer took up a position outside the door to speak to women before they entered the office. Judy and the other women scattered among the seated patients in the waiting room. The reek of death assailed Judy's spirit. As a neophyte, she felt her best contribution to the raging spiritual battle was to be silent and pray. The two other women contended for the souls and the babies of the seated mothers. The lanky Burnett sauntered up to the receptionist and quietly said, "Please stop the killing today."

The clinic staff seemed to suddenly explode from the walls. Clients were driven to back rooms and away from the help the rescuers offered. The office music was cranked up to an ear-numbing volume to cover the pleas of the rescuers. Their words of hope were engulfed by the screeching strains of "easy listening" music.

Judy and the others silently occupied the clinic waiting room for over two hours before she was handcuffed and led to the paddy wagon by police. After a brief rattling ride, she emerged at the Portland Justice Center, was taken inside, and booked. She continued to pray and sing praise songs in the holding cell at the jail until her husband, Gary, and her children picked her up. Judy was relieved.

Later that year, in Cherry Hill, New Jersey, she was one of over three hundred who were arrested as part of a training exercise for the planned Operation Rescue in New York City. Judy had not even considered approaching Gary with the idea of her going, but he sensed that she should go and told her he would finance the trip.

Shortly after Judy returned, Andrew Burnett was given a thirty-day sentence. Fearing the severe sentence might dampen her family's support, Judy decided to make future rescues a family matter. She concluded that she could accept nothing short of 100 percent support from them.

As she told her husband—and then each of her children—the news of Andrew's thirty-day sentence, it was as though they all repeated the same conversation: "Will you be going to jail?" they asked.

"That is possible, especially if I do more rescues. How do you feel about it?"

"Do you believe it is the right thing to do?"

"Yes," she said simply.

"You have to do what is right."

Judy's continued work on behalf of the unborn has produced spiritual growth in her children. Both have begged for the opportunity to rescue. But Judy and Gary are not prepared to risk state intervention in their family, so they have put a hold on the idea. Still, both now insist on attending the demonstrations that accompany the rescues. Eleven-year-old Christian has become an outspoken witness for Christ to the clinic escorts. He is undaunted by their overt hatred of Christianity. Christian says, "They are sinners like everyone else. They need Jesus."

Judy is pleased to hear him say this. It is what she has taught him.

"Our whole family is blessed," she says, "because we know that today there are children alive because of our efforts."

JUDY QUIRING

Artist for Life

A scream tore the air. Judy jumped out of the overstuffed chair where she had been attempting to watch television. The cry came from Grandmother. Judy sped down the staircase on the heels of her mother and followed into the bedroom.

The light was on in the bathroom. Both rushed in to find seventy-five-year-old Grandmother lying on the floor. Blood was spattered on the light blue tiled walls and pooled on the floor. Grandmother retched, and more blood soaked her clothes. Judy could hear her father in the next room demanding an ambulance over the telephone.

Grandmother appeared to be going into shock, but her concern was for the fear that registered on Judy's face. "Don't worry," Grandmother said. "I had tomato soup for lunch, and I just couldn't keep it down." It was a pitiful lie, but Grandmother's heart was behind it. Judy nearly burst into tears.

It seemed an eternity listening to the growling traffic outside their upper-middle-class Boston Brookline apartment before the whine of the ambulance arrived outside. The two burly attendants were dressed in white. One clearly carried the mantle of authority. "Your grandmother is very elderly," he said to Judy, "if we just make her comfortable and leave her here, she'll pass away during the night. But if we take her in, she might go through some terrible things at the hospital, and she's too old to be put through that."

Judy was shocked that someone would so boldly suggest surrendering Grandmother to death. At first, her mother acquiesced.

Grandmother, delirious from blood loss and having grown up in a generation where one went to hospitals only to die, was terrified. Her voice edged toward hysteria as she begged to be left at home. But Judy moved into the confusion. "No," she said. "You are professionals, and you will do everything you can to help her recover."

Judy could see that the driver's desire was for Grandmother to stay home and die. Grandmother's desire was to stay home and *live*. Even Judy's atheistic upbringing did not include a blatant death ethic. Strong family loyalty, a remnant of an earlier, more universal ethic of life, moved her conscience and her actions. So she insisted Grandmother be taken to the hospital where she could be helped.

Reluctantly, the men loaded Grandmother on the stretcher and bore her out into the cold, clear October night air to the waiting ambulance. Judy, her mother, and her father climbed into the rear and rode quietly to the imposing stone building. Inside the drab waiting room they alternately sat and stood for hours in ignorance of Grandmother's condition. Unknown to them, Grandmother had been examined and wheeled into surgery.

Hours later, the white-gowned surgeon emerged from between the swinging doors. "That is one amazing woman," he announced. "She has the constitution of a fifty-year-old."

Grandmother had been diagnosed with a peptic ulcer. The ambulance driver would have left her to suffer, but the doctor said, "She sailed through the operation."

Grandmother lived on for another dozen years—long enough to enjoy some of her great-grandchildren.

Judy's defense of life, however, did not extend to the unborn. In fact, she never even considered them. Her vision of the abortion issue was crowded with pregnant women. No space was allowed for the babies. "I was just quoting slogans that were popular at the time," she admits.

A year after Grandmother's emergency, twenty-four-year-old Judy became pregnant. "I could have had an abortion if I'd felt like it, even if it was illegal. I had the money," she says. "I was an atheist and pro-choice. But I got pregnant out of wedlock, and when it came down to the wire, I could not kill that baby. I was pro-choice until I got pregnant."

Judy spent that pregnancy in Maine, where her premature son was born—but soon died. "When I did lose that baby," Judy remembers, "there was a great sense of loss. But my family ignored the entire event."

Still, Judy clung to her outward support for abortion. "Even before I was saved, I knew abortion was wrong."

Several years later, *Roe v. Wade* was handed down. "I was happy," she admits. "I just thought, *That's great.*"

But almost ten years after the loss of her son, Jesus Christ found Judy wandering through her atheistic, feminist maze. Yet she still hung on to the outward confession of abortion rights. "I can't be too critical when I try to get church people going," she admits. "I'm sorry to say even after I was saved, for a long time I was not moved to do anything. It didn't seem to make a difference in my life. I was totally brainwashed into the mentality that I shouldn't force my morality on anybody."

After her conversion, Judy soon married, and it was through the loss of several more children through miscarriage that she relived the pain of her earlier loss. "Everyone was yelling at me," Judy recalls, "'well, you never knew it anyway. What are you crying about? What are you belly-aching about?'

"I realized that there's no place for a woman who has lost a baby to grieve," she says. "The world doesn't even accept that. I started to feel real remorseful, and I got to seeing that this culture hates children—and doesn't have much thoughtfulness for motherhood or women who miscarry or lose babies."

Judy's mind began to change on abortion. "The reason I came into pro-life still wasn't so much for babies. People tell me that I don't care for the women, but it's not true. I really grieve for them, and I want to help."

That sense of urgency grew stronger until late 1987 when Judy felt propelled into action. She located a southern Oregon activist, Myrna Shaneyfeld, and joined her in picketing and sidewalk counseling. Judy felt this was ideal because of her insight into the grief of losing children. Abortion-bound women, she felt, had no idea of the emotional toll they would pay for their abortions.

"There's nothing they can go through that I haven't been through myself, and that's where my heart bleeds for these women who are lied to. Nobody appreciates what the maternal instinct amounts to—and the loss suffered by these aborted women who suffer so horribly. I see how I've suffered *without* taking part in destroying a child, and I can just imagine what it is for women who go through abortion. The world keeps telling them, 'These are blobs of tissue. What are you crying about?' But I know better."

Myrna was headed for new avenues of pro-life work. It was a cold January night when they listened attentively to the tapes promoting the first Operation Rescue in New York. The fervent words of Randy Terry touched Judy deeply but she was not convinced. *I don't know,* she thought. *This looks a little radical. Maybe these people are getting swept up into some kind of Holy Roller thing—or is it something sensible?* She wasn't sure.

Myrna, however, was not new to rescues. The prospect of the nationwide rescue thrilled her, and she went. "Three of our gals went to the New York rescue," Judy remembers. "They came back to Oregon, and they were glowing. They could light up a room. There was just a life about them— such a fire—that I thought, *Boy, this is dynamite!* I didn't even learn until later that they had spent the week sitting out in the rain and walking for miles and going to some real fleabag hotel—and yet here they come back and they are glowing. It was such a spiritual thing to see them talk about it."

Being now convinced, Judy set her sights on attending the second Operation Rescue in Philadelphia. She and Myrna and several others organized fund-raisers to finance their trips. The rescues in Philadelphia were both clearly successful. In one, almost six hundred rescuers were present. Both clinics were closed for the day. "It was a good first rescue because it was so tame," says Judy.

But things were to be quite different in Atlanta later that year.

It was pitch dark as Judy's plane touched down at Atlanta's massive airport. The lights revealed its size but little of its character.

After a brief ride on the MARTA transit, Judy and the rest of the southern Oregon contingent were met by gracious local activists who lost precious sleep to drive them to the Motel 1 rescue headquarters.

Wanting to make herself useful the next morning, Judy quickly volunteered to fill her time behind the Operation Rescue registration tables. "I stayed back at the motel," she says, "and helped out with the people who were constantly coming in to register. The place was abuzz with excitement. People from all over the country were coming in."

Judy continued to register rescuers at the Motel 1 site during the prerescue rally. Soon a report came back from the rally that Randy Terry had been arrested for conspiracy to trespass. "I thought that was heavy," Judy remembers, "but kind of smiled because it wasn't going to stop anybody.

I had seen reports on the news that we were going to get fined $1,200, but it didn't make a difference to me. What did bother me was that it was scaring all of our families back home."

Judy awoke early the next morning to the chopping sound of the police helicopter overhead. The rescuers had slept scattered wall to wall in the motel room. Judy dressed in the tangle of other women in the room. As they left the room to face a sea of rescuers in the parking lot ringed by reporters, cameramen, and video crews, the surreal landscape was made more bizarre by the low-hovering police chopper.

Knowing the police intended to pick off any apparent leaders, Operation Rescue organizers secretly assigned crowd marshals. None bore any identifying mark, but each was assigned to about a dozen people for oversight. They all waited in prayer. "The funny part of it is," Judy said laughing, "since every single clinic was totally barricaded, it wasn't even possible to have the element of surprise. So, we just stalled there for hours because it was costing the city to have that stupid helicopter above whirring about, and we weren't even leaving. Andy Young sent that helicopter out there to watch us, and we were just standing there praying."

Soon, Judy was loaded with others into a van and taken to the MARTA. Bill Baird, a notorious East Coast abortion supporter, was in the station and reported the rescuers' movements by phone. As with any of her rescues, Judy's fears rose as the time approached. "I am terrified," she says. "All of these rescues are so different. I'm always scared to death."

When Judy and the others finally approached Atlanta SurgiCenter, there was mounting apprehension. "We were told we were going to get hurt," she said. "Randy Terry said, 'You might suffer a broken arm.' Then he said that courage is not the absence of fear, but it is doing what you know is right, even though you are scared to death."

The street before the clinic looked like an armed camp. Most of the police looked fed up with the whole thing.

Judy felt the asphalt bite into her knees as she got down on all fours. "Mike McMonigal was at the training session teaching us how to crawl," she explains. "I saw pictures that the police had staged to make it look like the rescuers were attacking them. So, to avoid that, they trained us to actually physically crawl so that it could no way be misinterpreted as an attack."

As soon as the officer addressed her, Judy went limp. "Either you stand up and cooperate, or we're going to have to hurt you. That's the choice you have."

Judy answered, "I'm sorry. I can't move because of the babies."

She didn't move. A hand clutched a clump of her hair and pulled her head back. The flash of the camera stung her eyes. Rough hands grappled with her arms, and she was dragged to the waiting white jail bus. "Now's your chance," they offered. "We don't want to have to hurt you any more, but if you don't cooperate, we'll have to."

Again they gathered Judy up like a bundle and heaved her aboard the bus, striking her head several times. She lay still. She had been tossed atop a pile of other rescuers in the rear of the vehicle. Eventually, they all found seats. "Everybody on the bus was crying. We were sitting there on our seats crying and singing, 'Paul and Silas went to jail, got no money for the bail,' at the top of our lungs."

When they arrived at the jail, the men and women were separated.

"When we were in jail the first night, it was really cold. After that, they put the heat on, but the first night was freezing." Like the other women, Judy received two blankets. They kept her warm for the night.

The next morning they were told that the men had given up their own blankets and had them sent down to the women. It had been so cold that they were concerned for the safety of the women. "I cried," she remembers. "These feminists don't understand how a group of Christian men and women can relate. These Christian men had enough respect for us that they would give up their blankets and stay cold for that night so that we could be a little bit more comfortable. These feminists don't know what they are missing."

Judy spent the next nine days in the Women's Detention Center in Atlanta, but in spite of her fear, she continues to see rescues as one of the best ways for her to save babies. "I think rescues are the only time in my whole life that I've been completely secure in the knowledge that I am in God's will," Judy says. "I've been to various churches where I've heard people say, 'When two or three are gathered together, I am amongst you.' I never felt the reality of that so completely as when you're putting your life on the line. There's a dimension that is indescribable. Within the fear, I know that this is where I'm supposed to be."

LAURA (ARMSTRONG) DUNN AND CAROL ARMSTRONG

Mother and Daughter Rescuers

"Today my mother killed me."

Those words planted the seed. Ten-year-old Laura Armstrong had listened intently as her mother, Carol, read *The Diary of an Unborn.*

It was still winter in St. Louis, but those last words chilled Laura the way no icy blast of the season could. It was 1973, and the U.S. Supreme Court had just legalized abortion.

The seed was buried deep in Laura's active, youthful life. But occasionally the baby's plight would appear in the periphery of her mind. All the while, the seed germinated—and grew.

A shoot abruptly surfaced six years later as she sat transfixed by the words of a sermon on Christians' responsibility to help others and how we should be helping to stop abortions. "It was as if God was speaking to me," Laura recalls, "telling me, 'Laura, you know they are killing babies, and you have a responsibility to do something to stop it.'"

Laura joined pro-life groups but was quickly dissatisfied with letter writing and handing out literature. Soon she added picketing to her pursuits. "I knew I had to go to the source," she says, "the place where babies were being killed." There was only one picket partner for Laura, but they diligently kept their lonely vigil during that cold autumn.

Laura still felt impotent on the picket line. She helplessly watched mothers enter the clinic—only to leave with wombs emptied. Laura wanted to go after them—to reach them—to hold them back—but her courage failed her.

It was a timely accident that led sixteen-year-old Laura to a rescue training session. Two rescues had already occurred in St. Louis: now another was planned. Local leaders plotted the steps of the mission. They assigned sidewalk counselors to care for abortion-bound women. All others, they insisted, must remain silent and prayerful. A training demonstration illustrated how rescuers were to go limp when police arrested them. "Going limp made sense to me," she explains, "because if I really believed babies were being slaughtered, I couldn't simply walk away when I was told since I would be the only obstacle in front of that baby's death. I realized later that the time it required to remove a thoroughly limp body was precious to our counselors' efforts as well."

Laura's excitement was contained only by the realization that she would have to approach her parents about this endeavor. It was hard to know what to expect.

Her father's face showed creases of concern when she unveiled the plan. Her mother concealed her fears. Both had stressed standing up for truth while raising Laura and her four siblings. Mother and father exchanged glances. Now was no time to start backing down on years of training. They consented.

St. Louis's third rescue began routinely when they entered the clinic. The soft music from the P.A. system and the lush plants in the hallways leading to the procedure rooms lent a nightmarish absurdity to the scene. Laura says, "It made me think of how music was played at the Nazi death camps. But soon the sense of evil was cloaked with peaceful prayer, and I knew the Holy Spirit was with us."

Police made no attempt to separate Laura from the adult rescuers, except that she had to be released to her mother. "After the booking process and being released to my mother," she remembers, "I returned home completely drained. Upon entering our living room, I recall I stared at my three-year-old sister who had snuggled up with a blanket on the couch. I knew I would be sitting in again. That evening I saw myself being carried out of the abortion mill on the six o'clock news."

Through the early part of 1980, the news coverage was good. Many pro-lifers joined the swelling ranks of the rescuers. Moved by her daughter's commitment and her own love for children, Laura's mother, Carol, took this as her cue and became active in picketing, sidewalk counseling, and crisis pregnancy work.

A major blow against the rescue missions struck at the end of April. The new Catholic archbishop, John L. May, openly opposed "arrest tactics," branding them "counterproductive and ill-advised." Pro-life spokesmen countered that rescues were not "tactics" but the actual saving of lives. But the press had seized on May's "counterproductive and ill-advised" line and intoned it repeatedly. There was a dramatic drop in the rescuers' numbers and support.

This setback, however, did not quell Laura's activities. As each abortion clinic obtained injunctions, rescuers moved to another one. The remaining rescuers would not give in. Laura and four others continued.

Laura also took on the responsibility for much of the work at a home for women with crisis pregnancies. Refurbishing the building and becoming the live-in staff member took a toll on her.

Carol expressed concern for Laura's overwork, but to no avail. Laura was driven by an inordinate power. Her desire to end abortion blind-sided her. She felt she should take on the whole job herself.

After an unsuccessful attempt to move her work to the

East Coast, Laura returned to her native St. Louis in July of 1982. Within a week one of her closest pro-life friends was found murdered, and her apartment was set ablaze. The case went unsolved.

That tragedy seemed to be the final blow for Laura. Her energy drained. In the ensuing months, her parents ministered strength to her but left her no room for self-pity. "I began to realize," she says, "that during this time God had not abandoned me. I had deserted Him by trying to control my own life and do things myself."

But the question of *why* about her friend's death haunted Laura.

Though she was physically recovered, the classic introverted symptoms of burnout hung on Laura like a pall. Over the next year, Laura focused on other things—most notably Greg Dunn. Greg seemed to infuse new life into her. Later they married.

Abortion was blotted from her life. "I didn't so much as want to hear the word *abortion*," she admits. "I was very comfortable in my own little world, and I didn't want abortion to invade my life."

Laura attended to her pregnancy and the birth of their first child, little Gregory. She tried to maintain an inward focus.

But the persistence of a small handful of activists returned Laura's mind to abortion again and again. Until this time, the St. Louis courts had treated the situation lightly and had not doled out any significant jail time. But when a number of rescuers were given up to five-month sentences, Laura was aghast. She knew that she must return to active duty. Her husband, Greg, knowing this would end her isolation, fully supported her reentry into rescuing. Laura's mother, Carol, also joined the rescuers.

Carol's choice came to her without warning. She was not usually the type to ask for signs from God, but she did pray that He would clearly show her whether she should become involved in direct action. Less than a minute after the prayer request, a refrigerator repairman rang the door-bell. His "little feet" pro-life pin caught her eye. When she asked about it, he took the invitation to speak. He explained he was involved in direct action and invited her to join. Carol became a regular in the rescuers' army.

In November of 1985, Laura, Carol, and another rescuer refused to pay the high cash bonds ordered by the court. The judge immediately jailed them. After they had spent a week in jail, Judge Goeke acquitted them on a technicality but warned them not to appear before him again.

Laura continued to rescue, though, even after she discovered her second pregnancy. Before particularly rough rescues, God seemed to intervene so that she was unable to attend.

Later, when this new child was nearly a year old, Laura and her mother were once again carted off to jail—sentenced to twenty-nine to thirty-five days. In jail, a young woman there for shoplifting came to them. She broke down and cried. She told them that she had been at an abortion clinic once before. Her boyfriend had brought her for an abortion, but rescuers had intervened and pleaded for her child. She and the young man had changed their minds about the abortion and left.

Laura's loss of her third child to a tragic miscarriage only deepened her compassion for the women who enter the clinics. She understands how completely a woman can suffer over the loss of a child.

She and her mother continue to see fruit from the work. "I know God always honors our faithfulness in saving lives," she says, "even when the results are not always apparent. One baby's life was saved because his mother saw a photograph in the newspaper of a rescuer being carried away by police. She had an appointment for an abortion, but instead she called our office for help. She said she changed her mind about the abortion because she figured if someone cared enough to get arrested for a complete stranger, she ought to care enough about her own baby not to have an abortion."

It is because of encouragement like this that joy still lives in the rescues of Laura and Carol. Their obedience, however, stems from another Source. "Our true leader is God," Laura says, "and He is calling Christians to join the battle all over the country."

DOW PURSLEY

Psychologist for Life

"Dr. Harrison, we just want you to know that Jesus shed His blood for your sins."

Harrison replied, "No, the babies shed their blood for me!"

Dr. Pursley's daughter, Melissa, repeated the exchange with the Fayetteville, Arkansas, abortionist to her father. The hardness of Harrison's heart amazed Pursley, and he wondered at the man's motives.

The abortion battle in semirural Fayetteville seems to be embodied in the two doctors. On one side, Dr. Dow Pursley, a counselor at the world-renowned Wheat Clinic, is gripped by the destruction of lives in abortion—both mothers and children. He is driven to the defense of life. On the other side is Dr. Harrison, who adopts a kindly media presence but is the area's undisputed champion—and profiteer—of abortion.

To Pursley, being pro-life is a natural component of Christianity. He feels that the Scripture is absolutely clear on the value of life in the womb. Back in 1973, while he was in Bible college, Pursley remembers being shaken by the news about the *Roe v. Wade* decision. "I knew it was murder," he says, "and I knew that my nation was in for trouble. But I didn't really know what to do, other than *be against it.*"

But there were small beginnings of the Fayetteville battle in Pursley's warm, inviting counseling room. At first Dow was puzzled by the emergence in women patients of post-traumatic stress disorder (PTSD), often suffered by Vietnam vets. He probed the sensitive psychic sores looking for a cause. None of these women had been in the unpopular Southeast Asian war. There appeared to be no common connection until, one by one, they began to reluctantly admit to having had abortions. The cold slab of the abortion table with gleaming chrome stirrups had been for each a personal "Vietnam."

Dr. Pursley launched a personal and professional investigation into the mental carnage he had found. He gleaned suppressed findings of post-abortion syndrome (PAS) from professional literature. Pursley was staggered by the implications. A little fact finding revealed that there were one million first-time abortions each year in the U.S. That meant there was a potential of well over ten million walking wounded from the abortion wars—and his *profession was in outright denial!*

Pursley carefully tracked seventeen of his own patients with PAS over a nine-month period. In that brief time he found it was the "anniversary reaction" to her abortion that caused one woman to require two weeks' hospitalization each year. Another was plagued with dreams of her baby crying—imploring her for a name. Others were less severe, but none were unscathed.

Up to this time, Dow's vocal opposition to abortion had been reserved for private discussion. In 1985, though, Dr. Pursley and some others arranged for activist writer Franky Schaeffer to speak in that area. The dramatic presentation stirred him to the front of the picket line before the clinic of Fayetteville, Arkansas, abortionist, William Harrison. Shortly after their pickets of the clinic began, on May 10,

1985, local activists appeared for a Mother's Day march in front of the abortionist's home.

To Pursley, picketing had been a bold step, and he kept that campaign aggressive—dogging Harrison's steps. But Dow was frustrated in his efforts to sidewalk counsel. The clinic sat so far from the road that the logistics prevented effectiveness.

One day, a weeping patient of Dow's revealed her embarrassing secret—her daughter had had an abortion nearly a year before. Though she had not even known of the abortion, the woman was wracked with guilt. Dow was deeply moved by her private agony.

But the agony had just begun. About a week later—on the anniversary of the abortion—the woman's daughter took her own life. "I determined at that time that I was going to be not just picketing," he says. "I was going to become more active."

Soon Pursley was presented with a solution. Shortly after the death of the woman's daughter, Dr. Pursley and his sixteen-year-old daughter, Melissa, were invited to attend the Pro-Life Action Network (PLAN) convention in St. Louis, Missouri, in April 1986. After hearing Joan Andrews encouraging direct action, Melissa informed her father that she intended to participate in the following day's rescue. Wouldn't he join her? He did. They were arrested along with 105 other activists. A fire was lighted in Pursley that day.

In August of 1986, Dr. Pursley carried his profession— both of faith and of vocation—to the battlefield. He walked onto the property of abortionist William Harrison and began to counsel an out-of-state couple who had just arrived. They stopped and listened. Midway through his counseling them, a policeman arrived. The uniformed officer informed Dow that he was trespassing and he would have to leave. Dow explained to the patrolman that he was in the midst of counseling and could not leave. His attention returned to

the abortion-bound couple. When Pursley was told he was
under arrest, he simply sat down on the walkway to the
front door and continued to talk to the pair. The frustrated
officer looked perplexed, then called for a backup to help
carry Pursley away. Since then, he and his daughter, Melissa, have been arrested several other times for front-door
counseling at the clinic.

Pursley's continued efforts in cooperation with other activists, the crisis pregnancy center, and local pro-life groups
have resulted in over one hundred babies saved in the last
two years. The area pro-lifers have arranged for most of
these children to be adopted. "But this guy [William Harri-
son] claims to do three a day," Dow says and adds that one
hundred is a "drop in the bucket compared to what he's
killing."

The city of Fayetteville has not been neutral in the continuing conflict. From the time the picket began, the council sought to quash the budding pro-life movement.
Enacting a ban on residential picketing, the city tried to
curb the focused demonstrations against Dr. Harrison. A
court battle ensued. Though the district court initially upheld it, the ordinance was later struck down as an unacceptable violation of the protesters' free speech. The
Fayetteville pro-lifers were awarded a cash settlement as a
result of their victory.

Soon Pursley's arrests took on the aura of harassment.
On a couple of occasions the arrests were not made until
long after the incident. Police burst into his office during a
counseling session at the Wheat Clinic, cuffed him, and
led him away—leaving behind a baffled patient.

Pursley feels that many abortion people are simply de-
ceived about the reality of abortion—falsely believing that
this is an issue of protection of women and their rights. But
he sees the engine that drives abortion: "It is the big-money
folks who are just exploiting women who are pregnant."

One former abortionist, whom he counsels, has told

him, "I had so much money, I would go out at lunch some-times, out of boredom, and buy a new automobile. Some-times I would leave in the afternoon, and I would fly to another city to have dinner. I had money coming out of my ears. I couldn't spend it fast enough."

Dr. Pursley also speculates about a more insidious motive for some abortionists. In his practice, he has seen some sim-ilarities between the mentality of abortionists and that of sexual perverts—particularly rapists. He contends that some are acting out aggression toward women by raping them with medical instruments. Many of his counselees have appeared to confirm this assertion. They have re-ported the rough, often very painful, way that abortionists treat them—as though they were being raped. Yet Pursley realizes that, like the rest of humanity, abortionists also need Jesus Christ.

Dow has counseled with a former abortionist from out of state who had done over ten thousand abortions. Haunted with dreams of trying to hide pieces of babies, he was driven from the business. The doctor and his wife have committed their lives to Christ. The wife is now very active in pro-life efforts, and the doctor has returned to other kinds of surgery. However, his former life has taken a heavy toll, and his confidence in his skills has been diminished.

In more recent events, the Fayetteville City Board has passed a new anti-picketing ordinance. Dr. Pursley and the other local activists make a point of challenging it with a monthly picket of Harrison's home. Police have made no arrests under the new ordinance, probably fearing another court challenge and another court-imposed settlement.

The pressures have only galvanized the pro-life move-ment around the area. There is little room for neutrality in Fayetteville. "No Christian enjoys breaking any law," Pursley says. "There are times when our conscience, how-ever, requires that we obey God's law when that higher law comes into conflict with man's law.

"The easiest thing to do for the unborn is nothing! I know, because I did nothing for years. The question is a hard one in light of Psalm 94 and Proverbs 24:11–12, because rescuing innocent blood seems to be every Christian's calling—just like being a witness is our job as Christians.

"The root problem is always sin! But you can't save a baby or a mother who is thinking about having her baby murdered by staying at home or in church. We must take our faith to the streets where it is needed.

"I have been criticized by many Christians and numerous pastors for 'taking the Bible too literally' on the issue of abortion and the Christian response to it. My response is the following: Not too many years from now, if the Lord tarries, I will die and then appear before the judgment seat of Christ. I have determined on that great day I would rather have the Lord say to me, 'Dow, you took My Word too literally,' than for Him to say, 'Dow, you took My precious Word and explained it all away.'"

DAN LITTLE

Randy Terry's Pastor

"Intellectually, I was sound asleep," said Pastor Dan Little when asked about his recollection of the 1973 *Roe v. Wade* decision. "I remember hearing about it, and I remember it meant absolutely nothing to me. I couldn't understand why it was such a big deal." This was not a proud admission coming from a pastor—the son of a pastor—who had grown up in the consistent, strong teaching of the Bible.

What could have happened to this man that would turn him from total apathy about abortion into the vibrant, excited minister of the Gospel who is often seen sidewalk counseling at the local abortion clinic today? And what would possess Dan Little to risk certain arrest just for a few more moments of talk with pregnant women in a clinic?

"It was not a 'Damascus' experience," Dan answers. "Probably back in about 1985, my awareness began to grow through the prayers of some of the people in my church who were praying—week after week after week—that the killing would stop. And the more I listened to them pray, the more I became convinced that what they were praying was the will of God and that abortion was killing. So it came on me that way. Only then did I begin to develop a philosophical stance about it from the Scriptures.

"I never felt any motivation toward activity—let alone, activism—until I began to hear people praying under the burden of God. More than anything else, it was just hearing them pray week after week at the midweek prayer meeting.

"Somebody's prayers woke me up, and they weren't even praying for me!"

However, as pastor, Dan was left with the quandary of whether or not to take a public position and support the pro-life activities of some members of his congregation. This was a serious step because one of those who have been praying was Randy Terry, a neophyte pro-life activist. Terry was one of the elders in Dan's church.

Terry and his wife had been picketing clinics—an activity that Dan considered unsavory. It was reminiscent of events of the early sixties—burning draft cards and protesting the Vietnam War.

"I had to decide," Pastor Little says, "whether I was going to give credence to what some of my people were doing—to give it support so that the congregation would back them and pray for them.

"That's up to a pastor. Any time that something happens in a church, or even happens in another church, if I stand in my pulpit and tell my people why I don't support it, by and large, those people are going to adopt my position.

"So I adopted the stance that I wholeheartedly supported them in what they were doing."

But God was not through with Dan yet. The next question he was required to answer was not as simple as the "support" issue. He faced, "Will I carry a picket sign?" This was a more difficult situation, and the pastor took quite a while longer to sort it out. He still viewed picketing with suspicion. But the rest of the questions came piling up faster than he could answer them:

"Will I pass out literature?"

"Will I go into an abortion clinic?"

"Will I refuse to leave if asked?"

"Will I get arrested?"

Dan's wife, Judith, cognizant of the Spirit's working on his heart, made these transitions beside her husband. The gravity of the issue was already clear to her.

Dan prayerfully approached each new question as he came to it, even the question of jail time. This looked like a particularly sensitive decision, but God was faithful and began to raise up support in the church.

In the early days of their pro-life activity in 1985, Pastor Little and Judith simply picketed on special occasions, like the anniversary of *Roe v. Wade*. But he perceived that his responsibility was greater than that. "Babies do not die on special occasions," he reasoned. "They died daily—bloodily and torturously and daily."

He and Judith and some of his church members began to commit time each week to picketing and sidewalk counseling. Without Judith's support, Dan feels that his efforts would not have been possible. She has taken a very visible role conducting press interviews and appearing on television to promote the cause of life.

But Dan did not stagnate. "I read up. I decided that they were actually killing children—they really were—and that God would honor it if I would go in there and speak on behalf of the children who were being offered up for murder.

"We planned a day, and we all went into the abortion clinic. We went around and started passing out literature to people to ask them to change their minds. And to plead with mothers who were there with their daughters, and boyfriends who were there with their girlfriends.

"Naturally, the staff came out and told us to leave. And we just said, 'We're not going to leave.'

"So finally the police came, handcuffed us all, and hauled us out."

The neighborhood's reaction to Dan's newfound activism was perplexing. He had operated a wholesale floral busi-

ness in the neighborhood for twenty-two years. He was
amazed to find that other businessmen were favorably impressed. Even the ones who were pro-choice responded well
to his willingness to go to jail for his convictions. Dan's
family and his own church firmly backed him. Eventually,
even Judith and twenty others of his flock were arrested. All
are facing certain jail time.

Pastor Little's first significant resistance came from some
leaders in other churches. These men would not confront
him directly, but it came back to him that they were disappointed in him. They thought Dan had scandalized the
name of the ministry.

To Dan, helping pregnant women *is* ministry, and *apathy*
is the scandal of which *he* had been guilty for years. This
ministry to the pregnant women began to bear fruit, but
Dan had not anticipated God's bumper crop—the one he
found in jail for the first time as he served his jail sentence.

Pastor Little saw these newly ripened fields in November
of 1987 when he was jailed for seven days. He had rejected
the offer to pay a fine for a rescue. He was booked into the
squalid jail, but he was in for the biggest surprise of his life.
"I just had a tremendous time there," Dan says. "All day
and into the night I was speaking to men directly about
their souls."

One of his fellow inmates had killed a man in a barroom
brawl. Dan reasoned with him from the Scriptures. The
man experienced a miraculous conversion to Jesus Christ
one week after his release. Pastor Little has been able to
follow up and help the man find a good job, and he has
assisted him in preparing for his marriage. He is not the
only man who is now saved through Dan's unique method
of prison ministry. Prisoners call him on an almost daily
basis. "My time in jail," Dan says, "has been one of the
high points of experience for me in ministry in my entire
life. I wish every pastor would spend a couple of weeks there
a year.

"I used to travel with a band and go to jails and minister, but there's been no other experience like being right there in the midst of the prisoners. They didn't even know I was a pastor for the longest time, but one by one God brought them my way.

"I talked with men for hours about how the Spirit of God wants to come over the darkness of their lives and move and bring order out of the chaos. I was just talking to them from the standpoint of how God wants to give them back the dominion of their lives. They've lost it—they've surrendered to a devourer—they've surrendered to someone who wants to victimize them."

But there was still more. In the midst of the flurry of ministry in the jail, during Dan's outpouring to his fellow inmates, God was able to speak to him with a very special understanding. Scripture was opened to him in a previously unknown way.

He describes the experience: "When I was in jail, I read through the Book of Romans twice a day. In the morning just reading and in the afternoon studying and taking notes. On one such day I read: 'All have sinned and fall short of the glory of God.' When I read those words, the Holy Spirit spoke quite clearly in my inner man saying, 'You don't know what that means.'

"'I'm a Baptist,' I protested, 'and I've known that verse all my life. I think I know what it means.'

"Still the Holy Spirit insisted that I didn't understand it in the way He was going to explain it to me. He drew my attention to the corrections officers [C.O.'s] and told me that they were deputized to express the authority of the sheriff over the prisoners. Then, in so clear and simple a way, the Holy Spirit explained to me that in the beginning God had deputized man to express His authority over the earth.

"Looking at Genesis 1:26, I saw that this was true: 'Then God said, "Let us make man in our image, after our likeness; and let them have dominion over the fish of the sea, and over the birds of the air, and over the cattle, and over all the earth."' In other words, God deputized Adam and Eve to exercise His authority. And the anointing, or His presence, in Adam's life was his badge.

"This is all clear in the New Testament as well. Jesus said, 'All authority in heaven and on earth has been given to me. Go therefore and make disciples . . . teaching them to observe all that I commanded you.'

"Ruling with God's authority, this was man's function in the Old Testament and it is still the function of redeemed man in the New Testament. Just as the heavens declare one aspect of God's glory, His handiwork, so man is to declare another aspect of God's glory, His authority.

"When man sinned, he lost the anointing, gave up his badge so to speak, and fell short or lost the ability of expressing the glory of God's authority. Thus, all have sinned and fallen short of the glory of God.

"From this brief but powerful time of having the Holy Spirit confront me with the Word of God, I have come to see these two things more clearly than ever. First, if active participation in sin causes failure to express the glory of God, then repentance and holiness are the cure. And who is so blind as to not see that God is purging the Church in America in order to bring her back to holiness? He wants to anoint—read, 'deputize'—her so that she is once again able to express the glory—read, 'authority'—of God over the earth. The early Church did it and so can we, when we begin to live in the same atmosphere of holiness that they did.

"Second, just as deputies must be on hand in the jail in order to express the authority of the sheriff, so Jesus commanded His Church to 'occupy' until He returns. No deputy can enforce the law if he is not on hand to do so. We're the deputies of the Lord; we, the Church, have been deputized to take authority over this abortion issue. The Church must do just what the C.O.'s do down at the jail. They physically bring the authority of the sheriff into the jail. And that's what we have to do in order to defeat the pro-death mentality that grips our nation.

"So long as we refuse to do it, all our talk is rhetoric. Imagine what would happen if all the sheriff's deputies did was sit around the office and send out bulletins to the prisoners. Imagine if they never enforced the law. The Church must occupy the abortion territory and stand there to express the glory of our Lord and Savior.

"What a time of glory I had there in that jail in putting this teaching to the test. God sent prisoner after prisoner to me, and to each one, I declared the glory of God. Two were saved, and more will soon follow.

"Occupying and declaring—it worked for me in jail. I believe it will work in the abortion mills throughout this land. So long as we don't speak for the innocent blood, the innocent blood speaks for itself—from the land. And we will be judged for it."

Dan now understands how God used jail to bless the lives of so many other saints and to bless the others through them. "I had a powerful time in there," he says. "I definitely am going back! There's no question about it!"

If there is no question of his going back, there is also no question about the route he intends to use to get there.

CATHY RAMEY

Blocking the Road to Dachau

The road to Dachau is deceptive.

The bus rolled through the lush green rolling hills—busy farms filling the vales between them. In the distance was a small group of buildings. Cathy could see the suggestion of a fence, but there was no icy finger that reached her soul to warn her of the numbing horror to come.

As the bus wheeled into the compound, the first hint surfaced. Even the barbed wire fences and guard towers did not convey the dour implications of the lifeless landscape that they enclosed. There was no tree—no bush—no blade of grass strong enough to struggle through the sterile gravel.

Cathy was guided to the first of the white plank-sided barracks. As she stepped from the warm spring air to the cool interior, her eyes were drawn to the photos of Jews with smiling faces who stood aboard trucks.

"They were being told that they were being taken someplace for their safety," Cathy remembers, "that this is good for them—that this is good for their society and their families are going to be safe. They bought into a lie."

As she moved along the photo gallery, the smiles were slowly extinguished. Cathy felt the cold shudder in her spirit as the haggard, hollow faces stared back at her from the brutal background of *civilized* Germany, circa 1940.

With mounting horror, she followed the photos and displays on their morbid trail of despair. At the terminus stood a stack of knobby, drawn bodies—fuel for the furnace.

The road to Dachau—for the Jews—had been deceptive.

Cathy would not finish the tour. She declined to go to the now silent, cavernous death mill. Some years earlier, she had immersed herself in Holocaust literature. She was all too familiar with what lay ahead.

The question remained, "Who could do such a thing?" The facelessness and bureaucratic barrenness of the assembly-line slaughter only deepened the atrocity. There should be passion—anger or hatred—in doing such things. There was none. There was only a sterile, calculated warehousing and disposal system.

The road to Dachau—for the German people—had been deceptive.

Several years later, Cathy sat in her sister's living room casually flipping through a magazine. Her attention was snagged by an article on antique furniture, which was her particular passion. Photos included several extraordinary pieces that took Cathy's breath away. She wanted them.

The article explained that these pieces had been part of confiscated Jewish estates during the Third Reich. They had been sold for a pittance. "I was envying the fact that I hadn't been there to cash in on that good deal," Cathy says. "I really had to admit that there was that potential for me to be just as lost as the Germans."

The thought had barely slipped through when the flush of shame rose on her face. She realized that *she* was capable of that kind of treachery. "It's just the grace of God that I wasn't in that situation," she says, "and I didn't have to make choices about whether or not to hide people and try and rescue them—or whether I would cash in on their estate."

The road to Dachau—for her—was deceptive.

That day's revelation gave new depth to Cathy's beliefs about the fallen nature of man. While in college, she had read of Jean Vanier's eccentric, but successful, experiment with a community for the retarded. She explains, "Vanier believed that by virtue of the fact that we're born into a fallen world, we're all wounded—in different ways. Some people are more overtly wounded than others. But we're all wounded, and we really need each other."

Cathy has experienced this kind of mutual aid in her work in a residence for the retarded. From them, she received the unconditional acceptance she had hungered for as a child. "The people that I dealt with," she says, "were so open and so honest. They would come up and give a big hug. I might get stiff as a board, but they never noticed. They never withdrew."

Sometimes, Vanier's influence has put her at odds with the prevailing wisdom of human service work. In her early work in the home, she resisted the "normalization" training designed to make retarded folks more publicly acceptable through behavior modification. In one particular case, the goal was to eliminate, what was to many, a visually offensive behavior of rocking—just sitting or standing, rocking back and forth rhythmically. It is a harmless activity that brings great comfort to many retarded people. Cathy was told that this behavior would publicly identify the retarded and leave them more open to discrimination.

Cathy felt that this approach was backward. The public, she felt, needed to be more accepting of people, even people with strange but harmless behavior. The "normalization" burdened the least capable people with the task of living up to others' expectations. The corollary was that "normal" people could not be expected to treat "different" people as fully human.

Cathy had heard of abortion. The graphic depiction of a

dismembered child she had briefly seen in high school lingered in the corners of her mind. But she resisted it whenever the vision assaulted her consciousness. "I honestly believed that abortion was something that you flew off to another state for—or a special hospital. It was something they did in Loma Linda, California, but *not* in Portland, Oregon. I was very naive."

Even when this idyllic view was shattered by reality, she took the passive stance. Interference, she felt, was unwarranted.

But God would not allow her the luxury of ignorance. Unwanted knowledge assailed her from every side, coming to her attention in the guise of other things. Ignorance was forcibly banished; apathy was finally sentenced to lifelong exile. Cathy's understanding of the painful reality grew; her involvement in pro-life work became deeper.

While sidewalk counseling at the ill-named Lovejoy Clinic in Portland, Oregon, she watched the stream of tortured young faces entering the clinic. Masking their guilt with modern myths, platitudes, and misinformation, the mothers-to-be-no-more scurried away from the pleading pro-lifers.

The road to the abortion clinic is deceptive.

The wind swept the darkened, empty street before the abortion clinic. It was the eve of the 1988 anniversary of *Roe v. Wade*. Next door, lights burned at the crisis pregnancy center for the all-night prayer vigil. Cathy listened intently as the two rescuers described the nonviolent tactics of closing clinics. Eagerly, she stowed away what they were saying. "Just the opportunity to listen to those women talking about placing their bodies to stop abortion was good," she says. "I was at a point where I had been going out and picketing and praying at the mill, and I was frustrated."

Cathy knew right away that this was the right thing to do. She could see the path of her action laid out before her.

She says, "It didn't seem like there was any justification for *not* doing it."

But her decision to join rescues only linked her to a more subtle war that lasted for months. "Before the first rescue," she recalls, "I went through a tremendous spiritual battle where I would say, 'God, I need to hear You on this.' But God didn't give me a flashing vision that this was what I was supposed to do.

"The night before the rescue, I went to the rally. As I walked to the rally, I was still trying to leave it open. And God was incredibly silent."

Cathy soon realized that God had already shown her what she should do—that she should obey what she had already heard. She was a little ashamed that she had tried to derive a spectacular experience as an answer to prayer. "It's making God prove Himself," Cathy says. "For Him to say in Scripture, rescue those being dragged to slaughter and take care of the widow and the fatherless, and then for me to have the audacity to say, 'God, You've got to prove that You really want me to do those things.' He said it in His Word."

So on the bright June Saturday morning before Father's Day, Cathy gathered with others for prayer in a quiet parking lot about a mile from the Lovejoy Clinic. She was fully prepared for the ensuing sedate ride in one of the cars or vans that approached the clinic from all directions.

The vehicles carefully parked a discreet distance away, waiting for the signal to converge on the building. Cathy's group had been assigned to the front door—one of the most used of the six entrances. The signal was given, and the group converged on the clinic to the astonished looks of the escorts.

Police arrived swiftly, and it was not long before Cathy and the other thirty-two rescuers were cleared away. But Cathy was not frustrated. She had obeyed, and she was confident that God would handle the rest.

Two weeks later, as she sat back at home after church, a blessing arrived. The Lord began to open up some of the plan He had engineered for her life until now. In Cathy's mind, He drew together memories of her deep interest in the Holocaust—all the volumes she had pored over—the memory of walking through Dachau—and her looking through the magazine at her sister's house. "It was like God was saying, 'I just trained you up.'"

The road to following Christ is well lighted, and Cathy is on it.

"Thy word is a lamp to my feet and a light to my path" (Psalm 119:105).

EDWARD ALLEN

Police Chief for Life

"I've spent most of my life protecting lives and property. That was my profession, and that's what I'm still doing. Only now I don't get paid; I get arrested," Edward Allen, retired police chief of Santa Ana, California, said to the steely-eyed Judge Kathleen O'Leary who was waiting to sentence Allen for entering an abortion clinic to save babies.

O'Leary paused in the quiet of the wood-paneled courtroom, looked down at the state's recommendation—a $15 fine—and said coolly to the most decorated police chief in the U.S., "One hundred twenty days." It was the longest sentence for trespassing in California history.

Allen didn't flinch. But a gasp rose from the assembled supporters as they realized the potential impact of the jail time on the seventy-eight-year-old's failing health.

O'Leary was adamant about the sentence. Pickets to protest the callous imprisonment appeared outside the Orange County Jail. Major political figures—Democrat and Republican—clamored for Allen's release while he wasted away, uncomplaining, in jail. Finally, a governor's order overrode the judge's dictum and freed the ailing lawman.

Chief Edward Allen had spent thirty-seven years in law enforcement, the last seventeen as the innovative, sometimes controversial, chief of the Santa Ana, California, Police Department. After his work for the FBI in the fifties, he became nationally renowned for having engineered the decimation of Mafia control in Youngstown, Ohio. A thorough researcher, Allen wrote a scholarly book documenting the existence of the Mafia long before even the FBI was willing to admit its presence. Allen is still considered to be the expert in the field and was used as a consultant in the movie of Mario Puzo's *The Godfather*. His tough but intelligent police style served him well in keeping Santa Ana's crime rate low. He retired in December 1972—scant days before the *Roe v. Wade* decision.

The chief's no-nonsense approach to crime did not mean that he was hardened. His personal interests reveal a tender Edward Allen, a writer of poetry and, after retirement, a lay minister to prisoners in the local jail. His thrice-weekly visits to the Orange County Jail to conduct Bible studies demonstrate his concern for the spiritual well-being of the prisoners.

Allen came from a "police family." The law had always been a very personal concern to him. He had gained a national reputation for rigid honesty and strict but fair enforcement of the law. Allen demanded that his men maintain personal as well as professional morality.

If there was anything that Edward Allen knew, it was the law. He had always known that just laws derived from God. To him, as with St. Augustine, it was a natural corollary that laws that defied God and His laws were no laws at all. So when he entered an abortion clinic to rescue babies for the first time in 1977, he viewed it as godly obedience rather than civil disobedience.

To Allen, abortionists were the people who should be arrested. He had personally ordered abortionists' arrests in Youngstown in the fifties and in Santa Ana in the seventies. During his last year as chief, he had the same abortionist arrested on four separate occasions. Allen's retirement, followed so closely by *Roe v. Wade*, only propelled him from arresting abortionists under the legal system to now seeking ways to arrest their grisly trade through other means.

Shortly after his retirement, he heard a local abortionist publicly claim that the morals of the community had changed and that the community now favored abortion. Angered by the lie, Allen single-handedly countered it by convincing the Santa Ana City Council to pass a resolution deploring the *Roe v. Wade* decision. From there, his activities extended to picketing to sidewalk counseling and finally to rescuing.

"There is no murder more premeditated than abortion," Allen says. This belief led him to treat it as first-degree murder in his actions as police chief and, later, as a pro-life activist.

Irony lurks in his voice as he recalls sending police officers out to arrest a physician who operated an abortion clinic in Santa Ana before the infamous *Roe v. Wade* decision. He says, "One of the officers who I used to send out to arrest the abortionist came to arrest me when I was sitting in at a Santa Ana abortion center. Abortion hasn't changed; I haven't changed; but the law has changed."

During the trial following Allen's third arrest, Judge O'Leary refused to allow him and his co-defendant, Ralph Buglione, to use the *necessity* or *choice-of-evils* defense, which contends that one may break a minor law to save a life. In truth, she allowed them no defense at all. She rejected all their witnesses and cut Allen short on testifying to his impressive credentials.

During the trial, the judge repeatedly stated, "This case has nothing to do with abortion." But abortion became a trial issue after the prosecutor sidled up to O'Leary and demanded that everyone in the courtroom should be forced to remove pro-life symbols. "It might prejudice the jury," the D.A. added. The judge ordered everyone to remove pro-life buttons or symbols during a recess and cleared the courtroom. When the court reconvened, Allen was still wearing his "little feet" pin.

Allen stood looking like a prophet with his white hair and beard. He refused to remove his pin. "This is a religious exercise," he said, "protected by the U.S. Constitution." O'Leary ordered him from the courtroom—until a Superior Court order overruled O'Leary's inordinate exercise of power.

But the pro-life movement, to date, has had little impact on the mounting slaughter of the innocents and the exploitation of their mothers. In his usual clear-eyed style Allen has assessed the flaws of the current pro-life movement. "Anti-abortionists have been arguing among themselves like a bunch of lawyers while children are dying," he says intently. "Four thousand abortions are committed every day. One unborn baby dies every three minutes. Unborn children are the poorest of the poor—who really need our help.

"It is important to help the hungry in this country and around the world, but at least the hungry can cry out. The unborn can't cry out for themselves. Talk is fine, but we need action. When your house is on fire, you don't write a letter to the editor about fire regulations. You put out the fire. Don't ever think we can ban abortion without serious self-sacrifice. We have to ask ourselves, Are we really against abortion? And if we are, why debate about it? You have to do something about it."

Chief Allen believes that those who march against abortion yearly in Washington, D.C., should simply continue their march to the U.S. Supreme Court building. He says they should return day after day and refuse to leave. Allen admits, though, that it will require self-sacrifice—the key to the Christian life. He points out, "Jesus commanded us to 'Follow Me'—and that path leads to the peak of Calvary."

Allen is deeply concerned for the United States and believes that its moral deterioration is due to a materialistic view of life. Allen's police work and now his pro-life work have adequately demonstrated to him that men's choice of money over morals is one of the earmarks of this century. "I have not one iota of a doubt that if this continues, we are through as a nation," he says.

In a poetic warning, written while in jail, Edward Allen illustrates the choice:

The Coin of the Realm

Wherefore is it written "In
　　God We Trust"?
Love is of God, love of
　　Mammon is Lust!
One can love God or love
　　Mammon, not both!
To whom do the covetous
　　render their troth?
To the root of all Evil: silver
　　and gold!
For thirty such pieces our
　　Savior was sold!!
Thus did the seller sell his
　　soul for hire:
Blood-money that poisoned
　　the soul of the buyer!

Would you sell your soul for
　　silver and gold?
Iniquitous Mammon "to
　　have and to hold"?
There is a distinction
　　betwixt Love and Lust,
Shall it be Mammon or God
　　whom you trust?

In the buying and selling of
　　life by abortion

Shall we acquiesce? What
      then is our portion?
If we are unwilling to die for
      another,
What then the price-tag for
      sister or brother?
If we in self-sacrifice do not
      agree,
What claim do we have to
      Christianity?
Would you offer Mammon
      your own child to kill?
Peruse the inscription ere
      you pay the bill:
"In God We Trust": would
      you render it Lie?
Have you no "Fear of the
      Lord" ere you die?
Disdaining God's Gift of
      Fear of the Lord
You forfeit the Hope of
      Eternal Reward!
Who plot Death with
      Mammon, in God do *not*
      trust!
By selling their birthright
      they crumble to dust
As *all* God's betrayers in
      Church and in State!
And lest they "Repent"—
      They merit such fate!

Are you image of Caesar or
      image of God?
The one whom you serve is
      the one whom you laud!

AFTERWORD

Dear Reader,

I close this book in the hope that you were able to find yourself among the pages. These people are no different from most of you readers. They have overcome the fear of risk to life, liberty, and sacred honor to "rescue those who are being taken away to death."

Surely, inaction is unacceptable in times like these. Just as surely, *more* than simple letters to legislators are in order. Someone would not write such a letter if a child were being killed in a neighboring house. Such a writer would certainly be judged irresponsible.

I have attempted to render these people "as they are" and to display their common humanity. They are not angels. Their stories reveal indifference, cowardice, insensitivity, rebellion, ignorance, and other common traits of fallen man. But, through God's grace, they have come to obedience.

Maybe some will think the events of these rescuers' lives are extraordinary. But it is not so. It is only in retrospect that we now see "connections" in their lives. Most of us rarely see these connections in our own lives. We are simply too close to them.

This brief listing of pro-life activists' tales by no means

exhausts the kinds of stories that I was told while writing
this book. Most rescuers have suffered comparatively little,
but some have paid dearly for our little brothers and
sisters—the least of these.

Certainly, not every pro-lifer suffers the same level of per-
secution. But there is nothing "safe" about this issue, nor is
there any option for becoming involved. If *we* do not, *no
one* will. The pro-abort attempts at intimidation will suc-
ceed *only* if pro-life activist numbers are small.

We shall all stand before the Judge regarding what we
have done. A requoting of the rescuer's text is in order, with
special emphasis on the latter parts:

> Rescue those who are being taken away to death;
> hold back those who are stumbling to the slaughter.
> *If you say, "Behold, we did not know this,"*
> *Does not he who weighs the heart perceive it?*
> *Does not he who keeps watch over your soul know it,*
> *And will he not requite man according to his work?*
> (Proverbs 24:11–12, emphasis added).

WHAT THEY SAY

This segment includes quotes from various individuals from both sides of the issue about abortion in general or rescue missions in particular.

Andrew Young—1968 civil rights activist arrested numerous times; 1988 mayor of Atlanta during Operation Rescue.

> *About 1968 March on Washington:* So it may be necessary for us to create such a disturbance in the system [that it] will either have to reform itself or destroy us. . . . Have a thousand people sitting around the Bethesda Naval Hospital so nobody could get in or out.

> *About 1988 Operation Rescue in Atlanta:* No comment. (From Neil Horton, Young's communications officer)

Hosea Williams—1968 civil rights activist; 1988 Atlanta city councilman.

> *About Atlanta's response to Operation Rescue:* I think what is happening now is just terribly un-American. It hurts me so bad that we who were leaders of the movement in the 50's, 60's, and 70's, are now the political leaders, and we are doing the same things to demon-

strators that George Wallace and Bull Connor and those did to us.

Alfred E. Moran—Executive director of Planned Parenthood of New York.

These people come from marginal and peripheral organizations, from people who are committed to more confrontational tactics than either the Catholic Church or the National Right to Life Committee.

Ronald Reagan—Former President of the United States.

Now, therefore, I, Ronald Reagan, President of the United States of America, by virtue of the authority vested in me by the Constitution and laws of the United States, do hereby proclaim and declare the inalienable personhood of every American, from the moment of conception until natural death, and I do proclaim, ordain, and declare that I will take care that the Constitution and laws of the United States are faithfully executed for the protection of America's unborn children.

Carter Hayward—Pro-abortion Episcopal priest and theologian.

Abortion would be a sacrament if women were in charge. Abortion should be a sacrament even today. I suspect that for many women today, and their spouses, lovers, families, and communities, abortion is celebrated as such—an occasion of deep and serious meaning.

Dr. James Dobson—Christian leader, author, and host of the internationally acclaimed *Focus on the Family* radio broadcast.

We are law-abiding people and do not advocate violence or obscene and disrespectful behavior, but to be sure, we *will* follow that higher moral code non-violently, to rescue the innocent, defenseless babies. And someday, the moral issues involved here will be as clear to the world as the Nazi holocaust is today.

Will Campbell—Veteran southern author and civil rights activist; University of North Carolina teacher of civil rights history.

Obviously, these folks are serious. They are presenting the issue of abortion in a way that I think will be hard to ignore.

An unnamed Portland, Oregon, police officer.

Arrest them? We've tried arresting them—and it doesn't work.

Denis Dillon—Nassau County, New York, district attorney.

I believe that peaceful, non-violent acts which might constitute such offenses as trespass and disorderly conduct, are morally justified when done to interfere with and prevent the imminent killing of human life by abortion.

New York Pro-Choice Coalition—In a flyer about Operation Rescue.

These people invade clinics, harass and assault women seeking abortions and doctors who provide them. They associate with people who have been convicted of bombing abortion clinics and kidnapping doctors.

Catholic New York newspaper editorial—May 5, 1988.

For their stand and the way in which they carried it [the rescue] out, they deserve our thanks.

New York Federal Court—To Operation Rescue and founder Randy Terry.

> Defendants Randall Terry and Operation Rescue are adjudged in civil contempt of this Court's May 4 Order and assessed coercive civil penalties in the amount of $50,000.00. . . . These funds are to be paid to plaintiff National Organization for Women and disbursed among the remaining plaintiffs according to its discretion.

Randy Terry—Announcing plans to bring Operation Rescue back to New York in the face of a court-ordered $50,000 penalty.

> "We must run to the lion's roar."

The Saltshakers—A self-described "evangelical think-tank" comparing rescues with the violence of abortion.

> We cannot condone violence on either side. On the one hand, we do not believe that laws forbidding trespass should be broken in order to stop abortion at various clinics. On the other hand, violence done inside of the clinics by doctors attacking defenseless life in the womb violates both Scripture and conscience. (National Abortion Rights Action League praised the Saltshakers position.)

Archbishop Eugene A. Marino, S.S.J.—Atlanta, Georgia.

> I would encourage people to give serious consideration to participation in Operation Rescue.

Margie Pitts Hames—The Atlanta, Georgia, attorney who fought and won "abortion rights" before the U.S. Supreme Court in *Doe v. Bolton.*

> There's never been an injunction sought by any of the

abortion providers here. . . . We do not harass [the demonstrators]. We respect their rights. . . .

They have a right to demonstrate—the question is, "Why don't they respect somebody else's rights?" They think their rights are superior to the woman's right to safety, the clinic's right to be open and operate as a constitutional and legitimate business.

It's the arrogance of the movement—and their self-righteousness—that is quite offensive to me. . . .

I think there's a total lack of respect for women in all of this.

Mother Teresa of Calcutta—Speaking in Philadelphia, Pennsylvania, August 6, 1976.

A nation that destroys the life of an unborn child, who has been created for living and loving, who has been created in the image of God, is in a tremendous poverty. For a child to be destroyed because of the selfishness of those who fear they may not be able to feed one more child, fear they may not be able to educate one more child and so decide that the child has to die—that's poverty.

Nat Hentoff—Editor of the liberal *Village Voice* newspaper.

Before the Civil War, abolitionists were arrested and jailed for acting on their conviction that blacks were fully as human as everyone else—and that they must have Constitutional rights. The pro-life activists—as in the rescue movement—are the abolitionists of this century, acting on their conviction that developing human beings have the same right to live as those of us who are already born.

Rev. Jerry Falwell—Pastor, preacher, and founder of the Moral Majority.

Non-violent civil disobedience is the only way to

bring an end to the biological holocaust in this country.

Lynne Randall—Atlanta, Georgia, abortion clinic director
to pro-life rescuers as she tried to give them handfuls of
condoms.

If you really wanted to do something about abortion,
you'd use and distribute these.

B. D. Colen—Pro-abortion columnist writing in November
8, 1988, *Newsday*.

No, the question being asked about Operation Rescue
shouldn't be, "Why are these people doing this?"
Rather, it should be, "Why has it taken them so long
to get to this point? Where have they been?"
    Beyond that, one has to wonder where the rest of
the anti-abortion movement has been hiding. . . . it
seems to me, at this time, Operation Rescue is clearly
where the rest of the anti-abortion movement should
be.

God—In Proverbs 24:10–12.

If you faint in the day of adversity,
    your strength is small.
Rescue those who are being taken away to death;
    hold back those who are stumbling to the
        slaughter.
If you say, "Behold, we did not know this,"
    does not he who weighs the heart perceive it?
Does not he who keeps watch over your soul
        know it,
    and will he not requite man according to
        his work?

A RESCUE GLOSSARY

Abortuary—An abortion clinic; also called death mill, killing center, death camp.

Baby Doe Rescue—A rescue where participants identify themselves with the defenseless and nameless victims of abortion by giving their names to police as "Baby John Doe" or "Baby Jane Doe."

Covert (accent on first syllable)—A pro-life person who makes an abortion appointment for the day of a planned rescue to ensure the clinic will be open.

CPC—An acronym for a crisis pregnancy center, a place where pregnant women will find help and alternatives to abortion, i.e., medical care, housing, clothing, friends.

Crowd Marshals—Designated persons who help direct rescuers and maintain peaceful and prayerful decorum during large rescue missions; they are usually identified by armbands.

Direct Action—Nonviolently blocking the entrances to abortion clinics or peacefully occupying their rooms in order to stop the killing.

Doe v. Bolton—Companion legal case to *Roe v. Wade*. Bolton prohibited state restrictions on late-term abortions. Case was argued and won by Atlanta attorney, Margie Pitts Hames.

Escort—A person who acts on behalf of an abortion mill to prevent abortion-bound mothers from hearing or receiving information from sidewalk counselors. Escorts lead the women into the clinic; also called deathscorts. See *Pro-abort*.

Flex-cuffs—Plastic strapping designed to form binding loops. Used by police to replace regular handcuffs during mass arrests.

Go Limp—To slacken the muscle tension throughout the body in order to become "dead weight." Increases difficulty for police attempting to move the rescuer to a paddy wagon. This tactic delays the clinic's opening and, thus, the deaths of babies. It entails no actual resistance to arrest; sometimes called passive resistance.

Lock Arms—Rescuers lace arms together and form a human chain. The only time rescuers are instructed to stand is when an abortion-bound mother tries to pick her way through seated rescuers. Those near the door stand and lock arms but offer no violence; also called link arms.

Lock 'n' Block—A rescue mission with a number of people using a combination of chains, bicycle locks, cement blocks, and other objects along with their bodies to block clinic doors or occupy abortion rooms.

Necessity Defense—A legal defense contending that the act of a defendant was necessary to bring about a greater good, i.e., trespassing to save life or property from a fire; also called choice-of-evils or greater good defense.

Nonviolent—The actions and attitudes in which rescuers do no hurt or damage to persons or property. Deliberate attempts by rescuers to avoid *even the appearance* of a threat.

NOW—An acronym for National Organization for Women, a pro-abortion political group.

Operation Rescue—A series of organized national rescue missions held in various U.S. cities.

Pain-compliance—Painful holds used by police to force rescuers to walk to paddy wagons and jail buses; also called come-along holds.

Peaceful—The attitude and action of rescuers who refuse to present verbal or emotional abuse to opponents or police.

Picket—To legally demonstrate for or against something by carrying placards.

Plant—A pro-abort woman who pretends to be an abortion-bound woman and is escorted into the clinic.

Post-abortion Syndrome (PAS)—The psychological dysfunction experienced by women who have had abortions; symptoms resemble the post-traumatic stress disorder suffered by many Vietnam vets.

Pro-abort—Short for pro-abortionist; a person who favors abortion; particularly used of those who actually assist the work of the aborturaries by serving as escorts, spokespersons, or counterdemonstrators.

Pro Bono—A Latin designation for legal work offered without charge by attorneys.

Pro Se—A Latin designation for a legal defendant who chooses to mount his own defense.

Psalter—A booklet of prayers, affirmations, psalms, and songs that rescuers and supporting demonstrators recite or sing together during a rescue mission.

Rescue—Obedience to Proverbs 24:11–12; to prayerfully, peacefully, and nonviolently place your own body between the victims (mother and child) and the killers (abortionists).

Rescue Mission—A planned event where pro-life people attempt to stop abortions with the concerted efforts of prayer, demonstrating, sidewalk counseling, and blocking doors (or occupying rooms) at the abortion clinic.

RICO—An acronym for the Racketeer-Influenced and Corrupt Organizations Act; special laws used to indict organized crime figures and confiscate their criminal profits. RICO charges have been filed against a number of pro-lifers and their organizations.

Roe v. Wade—The U.S. Supreme Court decision on January 22, 1973, that legalized abortion in all nine months of pregnancy.

Sidewalk Counselors—Persons who place themselves outside the abortion clinic seeking to talk to abortion-bound mothers and plead for the lives of their children. These counselors are integral to any rescue mission.

Siege of Atlanta—The second phase of Operation Rescue in Atlanta, Georgia, which took place October 3–8, 1988.

Skooch—Lateral movement by the rescuers while in a seated position.

PRO-LIFE ADDRESSES AND PHONE NUMBERS

The following list includes pro-life direct action groups. These people need your prayers, your financial support, and your active presence to do their lifesaving work. Contact them immediately. Please help.

Operation Rescue or Project Life
P.O. Box 1180
Binghamton, NY 13902
(607) 723-4012

Operation Rescue/Atlanta
P.O. Box 675439
Marietta, GA 30067-0015
(404) 421-9552

Advocates for Life
P.O. Box 13656
Portland, OR 97213
(503) 257-7023

Defenders of Life
P.O. Box 320
Drexel Hill, PA 19026

Feminists for Life
811 E. 47th Street
Kansas City, MO 64110
(816) 753-2130

Life and Family Center
601½ Mall Germain, Suite 201
St. Cloud, MN 56301
(612) 252-2526

Life Support Services
P.O. Box 16849
San Antonio, TX 78216
(512) 662-7334

Pro-Life Action League
6160 Cicero
Chicago, IL 60646
(312) 777-2900

Houston PLAN
2470 S. Dairy Ashford, #166
Houston, TX 77077
(713) 578-7044

Pro-Life Coalition of Southeast Pennsylvania
247 Keswick Avenue
Glenside, PA

Pro-Life Direct Action League
P.O. Box 35044
St. Louis, MO 63135
(314) 863-1022

Pro-Life Non-Violent Action Project
P.O. Box 2193
Gaithersburg, MD 20879
(301) 774-4043

Whole Life Ministries
P.O. Box 5957
St. Louis, MO 63134
(314) 428-6662

Pro-Life Action Ministries
1163 Payne Avenue

St. Paul, MN 55101
(612) 771-1500

California Operation Rescue
2464 El Camino Real
Number 158
Santa Clara, CA 95051
(408) 984-7233 or
(209) 538-6419

East Bay Area Rescuers
San Francisco, CA
(415) 283-7097

Washington State Operation Rescue
P.O. Box 4124
Wenatchee, WA 98807

THE RESCUER'S
AGREEMENT

I understand the critical importance of rescue operations be-, ing unified, peaceful, and free of any actions or words that would appear violent or hateful to those watching the event on TV or reading about it in the paper.

I realize that some pro-abortion elements of the media would love to discredit this event (and the entire pro-life movement) and focus on a side issue, in order to avoid the central issue at hand—murdered children and exploited women.

Hence, I understand that for the children's sake, this gathering must be orderly and above reproach.

Therefore . . .

1) As an invited guest, I will cooperate with the spirit and the goals of the rescue as explained in this pamphlet.

2) I commit to be peaceful and nonviolent in word and deed. I will not raise my voice in anger, or to make any threatening gesture, action, or statement, even if I am violently attacked either physically or verbally; but will follow the example of Christ.

3) I will follow the instructions of the rescue crowd control marshals.

4) Should I be arrested, I will not struggle with police in any way (whether in deed or in tongue), but will remain

polite and passively limp, remembering that mercy triumphs over judgment.

5) I understand that certain individuals will be appointed to speak to the media, the police, and the women seeking abortions; I will not take it upon myself to yell out to anyone, but will continue singing and praying with the main group as directed. I sign this pledge having seriously considered what I do with determination and will to persevere by the grace of God.

Signature:

Date:

ABOUT THE AUTHOR

Paul deParrie is a pro-family, pro-life activist. A father of six, he is a former pastor, street minister to prostitutes, and director of an antipornography group. He has co-written one other book, *Unholy Sacrifices of the New Age* (Crossway, 1988), with Mary Pride.

COLOPHON

The typeface for the text of this book is *Goudy Old Style*. Its creator, Frederic W. Goudy, was commissioned by American Type Founders Company to design a new Roman type face. Completed in 1915 and named Goudy Old Style, it was an instant bestseller. However, its designer had sold the design outright to the foundry, so when it became evident that additional versions would be needed to complete the family, the work was done by the foundry's own designer, Morris Benton. From the original design came seven additional weights and variants, all of which sold in great quantity. However, Goudy himself received no additional compensation for them. He later recounted a visit to the foundry with a group of printers, during which the guide stopped at one of the busy casting machines and stated, "Here's where Goudy goes down to posterity, while American Type Founders Company goes down to prosperity."

Substantive Editing by Michael S. Hyatt

Copy Editing by Dimples Kellogg

Cover design by Kent Puckett Associates, Atlanta, Georgia

Typography by ProtoType Graphics, Inc., Nashville, Tennessee

Printed and bound by Maple-Vail Book Manufacturing Group, Manchester, Pennsylvania

Cover printing by Weber Graphics, Chicago, Illinois